The Glories
of cross stitch

The
Glories
of cross stitch

Lauren Turner

CIMA BOOKS

London

First published in Great Britain in 2000 by Cima Books
32 Great Sutton Street
London EC1V 0NB

Copyright © Cima Books 2000
Text and charts copyright © Lauren Turner 2000

10 9 8 7 6 5 4 3 2 1

A CIP catalogue record for this book is available from the British Library

ISBN 1 903116 06 6

Designed by Sara Kidd
Edited by Ian Kearey
Photography by Shona Wood
Illustrations by Kate Simunek

Reproduction by Bantam Prospect, Essex
Printed in the United States

Contents

Introduction

As a child of seven at school I remember being fascinated by my introduction to 'sewing'. With Aida fabric (eight holes to the inch), bulky thread and huge needles we were taught the simple running stitch, zigzags and the basic cross stitch. In this respect, we were part of a long-standing tradition: children in eighteenth-century orphanages also learned cross stitch, although they used silk or wool on very fine fabric. With these skills, they created alphabet samplers which continue to inspire generations.

The orphans were expected to create examples of their stitching in order to gain a place as a servant in a household where their skills could be employed. Today, surviving examples of their work can be found in museums and sale rooms, bearing witness to a period of hard times for deprived children. Some of the samplers are signed and dated by children as young as six – a poignant and humbling chronicle of their lives.

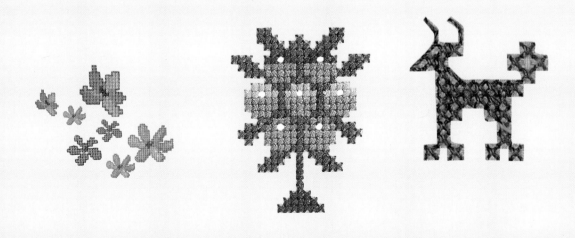

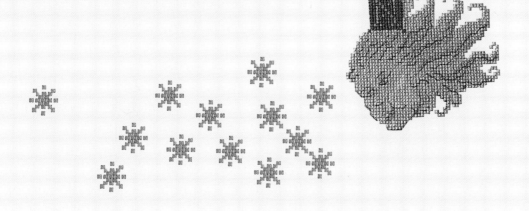

These children's skills were cultivated to a level far exceeding anything expected from young people today. The charming appeal of these samplers lies in their decorative simplicity, which will continue to be enjoyed by future generations.

The real fascination of cross stitch lies in its sheer simplicity. It is accessible to stitchers of all ages and all levels of ability. One stitch is used over and over again, either in a pattern or in a variety of colours to build up an image. Cross stitch is easy and addictive, and this single stitch can be used to create anything from a simple motif to a finely detailed piece of embroidery .

Whenever I work on a new piece, the magic of watching it grow before my eyes never fails to excite me; it makes it hard to put down without doing 'just a little bit more'. A little love and devotion applied to these techniques will create treasures that can be passed from one generation to another.

Techniques

One of the most attractive aspects of cross stitch is that the actual range of techniques required to begin is relatively small, and you can see progress from the very first stitch. The more you practise the more you will discover, and you will build up a repertoire that suits your projects and your way of working.

'When love and skill work together, expect a masterpiece'
John Ruskin

This first section of the book introduces the basics of cross stitch and takes you through the techniques and methods that you need to make the samplers in the projects. In the projects themselves specific instructions for each piece are included, along with a chart, directions for thread make and colour, and any other relevant information.

Needles

The size of needle you choose is really a matter of personal preference. The projects in this collection use either a size 22 or 24 blunt-ended tapestry needle. The smaller the number, the smaller the needle. It is common practice to use a size 24 needle on 14 count Aida or 27 count Linda, and a size 22 needle on 18 count Aida.

Cotton and fabric

Stitchers are advised to use the exact shades of stranded cottons listed for each project in order to maintain the delicate balance of colour which has been achieved in the illustrations. The makes recommended are DMC, Anchor and, in some cases, Madeira, all of which are widely available from good-quality outlets.

The samplers featured have generally been stitched on ivory or coloured Aida or Linda fabric – they will also look fine on natural linen. The smaller projects are suitable for children using 11 count Aida.

Using the charts

Each square on the charts represents one cross stitch worked over one square of Aida fabric (or two threads of evenweave fabric). There are heavier lines every 10 stitches to make counting easier. The number of strands that each design uses is specified in the text.

Sizes

In the projects, sizes are given for the area of the actual design, together with a reminder to allow extra fabric for the borders. Allow 3–5cm ($1\frac{1}{8}$ – 2in) on all sides, depending on the size of the project. To calculate the size for different fabrics, count the number of stitches in the design and then divide by the number of threads per centimetre (or inch) in the chosen fabric.

Separating strands

Stranded cotton comes in six strands which need to be separated singly and recombined in order to get even coverage. To do this, hold up one end of the thread and pull a single strand straight up until it is separated from the rest.

Project thread is most easily kept on a thread organizer. This can be easily made from a strip of card with enough holes, punched with a hole puncher, down one edge to correspond with the number of colours used on a project.

Cut the thread into 51cm (20in) lengths. Mark the symbol for the first colour beside the top hole and loop the thread into that hole. Repeat for each colour to be used in the colour key. Pull out one length at a time.

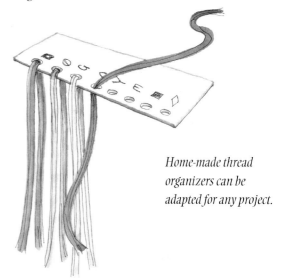

Home-made thread organizers can be adapted for any project.

CROSS-STITCHING

All top stitches should lie in the same direction to create a uniform appearance. Stitches can be formed in two ways:

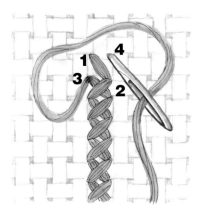

Method A completes each stitch in turn.

Method A – by completing one cross at a time (see above), which is essential where stitches are scattered. Bring the needle up at 1, down at 2, up at 3, down at 4, and so on.

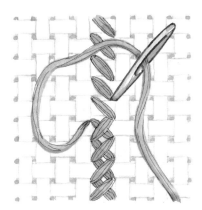

Method B completes the crosses in rows.

Method B – by travelling along a vertical or horizontal row to form the first half of the stitch and then travelling back to form the second half (see above).

Use these two stitching methods according to the layout of stitches and personal preference. Method A will create a bulkier fabric overall because more thread is used at the back of the fabric. Method B is only possible where there are several adjacent stitches of the same colour. It uses less thread and thereby ensures a more pliable fabric overall; however, this method can result in a ridged line of stitches, so take care when using it. Aim to stitch in a direction that will minimize any thread bulk at the back of the fabric.

Note that left-handed stitchers should mirror the diagrams when stitching.

SECURING ENDS

When starting a project or working in a new area, begin by placing your finger over 1cm (³/₈in) of thread at the back of the fabric and securing with the first few stitches.

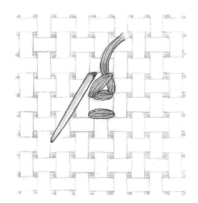

Secure the thread with the first few stitches.

Where there are already cross stitches, weave your needle under these at the back and hold until the first stitch is complete.

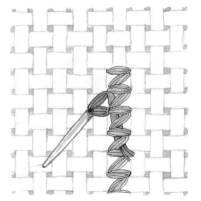

Weave the needle under the cross stitches at the back of the fabric.

When finishing a thread, weave it under the stitches at the back for at least 1cm (³/₈in) before snipping it off. Never secure with a knot, because this will cause bulkiness in the finished fabric.

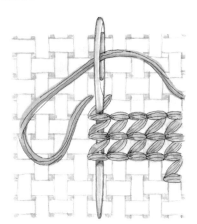

Weave at least 1cm (³/₈in) when finishing to secure the thread.

FRENCH KNOTS

Decorative French knots are not difficult to produce, and can add an extra touch to your work. Bring the needle up to where the knot is to be positioned. Hold the thread taut and place the needle behind it.

Twist the thread once around the needle, then push the needle back into the same place while holding the thread taut. Pull the needle through to form the knot.

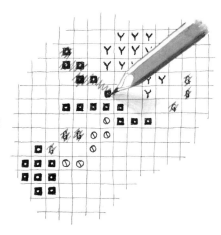

Shade in the chart as you complete the stitching.

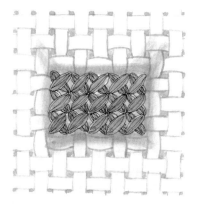

To stitch a French knot twist the thread once round the needle.

When working French knots, make sure you do not pull the needle too hard, or the whole knot may be taken through the fabric and you will have to begin the whole process again – a lot of work for a simple technique!

TIPS FOR CREATING FINE STITCHING

Correct tension is the great secret of success in fine cross-stitching; pulling too tight will result in puckering of the fabric and will therefore spoil the overall finish. Allow just enough to create a 'rounded' stitch without looping.

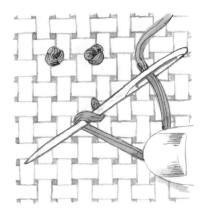

Pulling too tight will make the fabric pucker.

Shade the chart with a pencil as you complete the stitching, to make it easier to keep your place and keep up with your overall progress.

Twisted threads cause the fabric to bulk up so allow the thread to untwist after every few stitches.

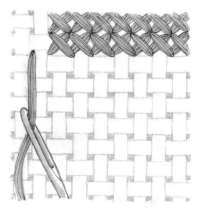

After every few stitches let the needle hang to untwist the thread.

Avoid carrying the thread across the back of the fabric for more than a few stitches; it should be caught into the back of stitches. The reverse of the piece should be as neat as possible, with no dangling ends because these are likely to show through to the front of the finished piece. Use stitching method B (see above) as much as possible to use less thread at the back and thus create a more even finish.

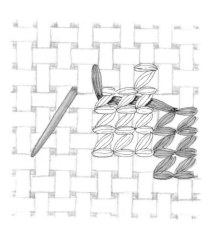

To take thread across the back, link it through existing stitches.

BACKSTITCH

Backstitch is used for outlining and fine detail, and should be added after the cross stitches are complete. Bring the needle up at 1 and down at 2, up at 3 and down at 1, up at 4 and down at 3, and so on.

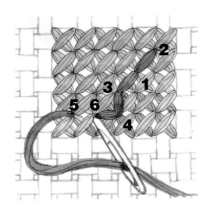

For a smooth, even line, work backstitch over two squares.

Pay special attention to the tension on the non-diagonal stitches (e.g. 3–4, and 4–5), because these can 'disappear' between stitches if they are too taut, especially when using a single thread. Work backstitch over two squares to get a more fluid line.

LIGHTING

When using threads of similar hues, replace the halogen light bulb in your working light with a daylight simulation light bulb. Daylight bulbs give a bluish light like natural north light; this allows for perfect colour matches and is restful on the eye when doing close or intricate work. The bulbs can be purchased from good art and craft stores, and daylight-simulation fluorescent tubes are also available.

FINISHING

Begin by removing any remnants of centre markers. Then hand-wash the project in lukewarm suds to increase the bulk of the stitches and to maximize the sheen in the threads, squeezing gently, without rubbing the fabric. Rinse thoroughly, squeeze but do not wring, then spread flat until half dry.

To press, lay the damp embroidery on thick towels and press the reverse lightly to 'raise' the stitches and to remove any puckering in the fabric. Continue until all moisture has evaporated and all creasing is removed. The fabric is now ready for mounting.

MOUNTING

Cut acid-free mounting board to fit within your chosen frame, allowing room for the fabric to wrap around the edges. Lay the embroidery face down and place the mounting board over it. Pin the fabric to the edges of the board. Keep checking the front and

carefully adjusting it until all the edges appear straight. Use a strong thread to lace across the back from side to side at 2.5cm (1in) gaps. Repeat this procedure on the other two sides; to finish, fold the corners flat and secure them by stitching.

Pin the fabric to the edges of the mounting board.

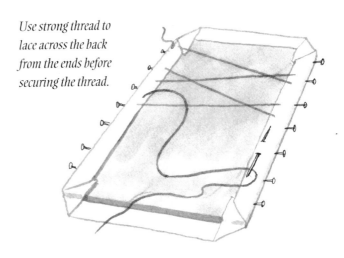

Use strong thread to lace across the back from the ends before securing the thread.

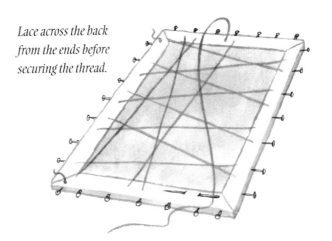

Lace across the back from the ends before securing the thread.

CELESTIAL SPHERES

Heaven and earth in cross stitch: the mysteries of the universe, including astrology and astronomy, provide the inspiration for this collection of designs. The beauty of the stars and the night sky makes us wonder at the awesome scale of our solar system and beyond. How much, or how little, do we know of the universe – and how much more is there still to learn?

Sun, Moon and Stars

This design celebrates the radiant beauty of the heavens and the harmony and order of the universe. The balance is between the warmth of the sun and the guiding light of the moon.

Design area (approx): 24 x 25cm (9½ x 10in) on 14 count ivory Aida

Design size: 137 x 128 stitches. Allow for borders when cutting fabric.

STITCH AS FOLLOWS:

Use two strands of thread unless specified (S) = single strand. Backstitch is represented on the chart by a straight line (see Techniques, page 8).

1 Begin the sun motif at the centre and work outwards. Place the borders.

2 Add backstitch to the stars.

BACKSTITCH COLOUR:

Stars (S) metallic gold (see below)

3 Personalize with your own initials and date, using Alphabet 1 (see page 122).

USING METALLIC THREAD

Take one strand of thread and fold it in half. Thread the fold through the needle and then pass the needle through this loop and tighten; you now have enough thread attached to the needle to avoid slipping. Work a little more slowly to ensure that the thread sits neatly without looping.

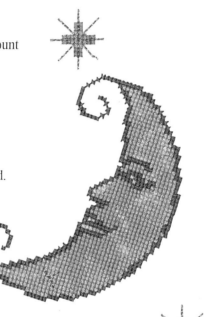

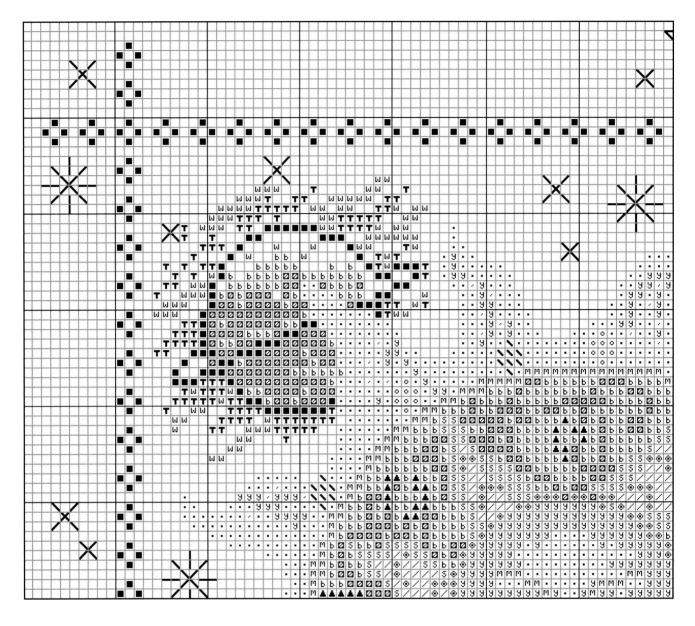

KEY

◣ Peacock blue – medium	DMC 807	♣ Lilac – light	Anchor 108
○ Aquamarine	DMC 958	Ϻ Blue mauve – very light	DMC 3747
T Turquoise – light	DMC 598	⊙ Metallic mauve – very light	DMC 3743
⨆ Willow green tint	DMC 369	⋁ Pearl pink – very light	DMC 963
◌ Baby blue – very light	DMC 775	▩ Peach – light	DMC 353
ᑓ Antique blue – very light	DMC 3752	P Salmon	DMC 3341
⊠ Sky blue – medium	DMC 813	╱ Coral pink	DMC 351
ϑ Sun orange	DMC 742	S Indigo blue – dark	DMC 792
▪ Soft gold	Anchor 311	⊛ Blue mauve	Anchor 118
⸴ White			
✕ Metallic gold	Madeira 5		
■ Royal blue – dark	DMC 796		

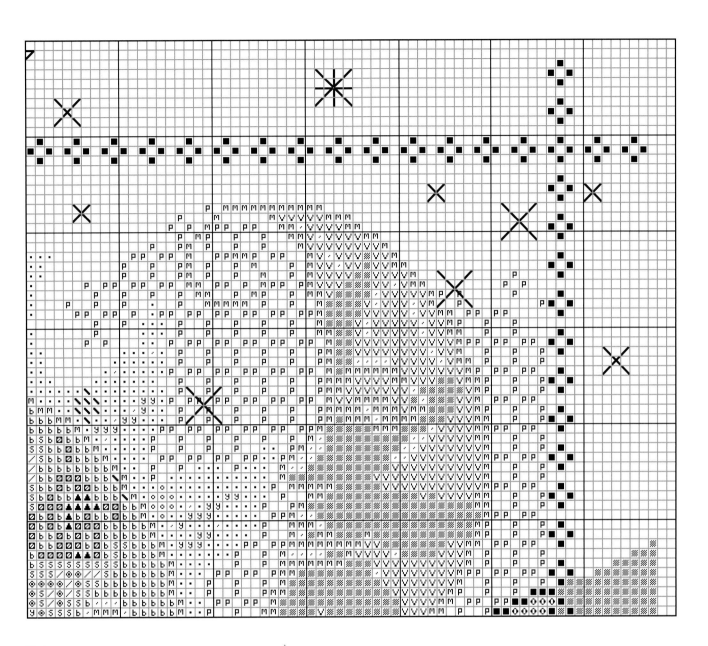

KEY TO CHART DIVISION

page 16	page 17
page 18	page 19

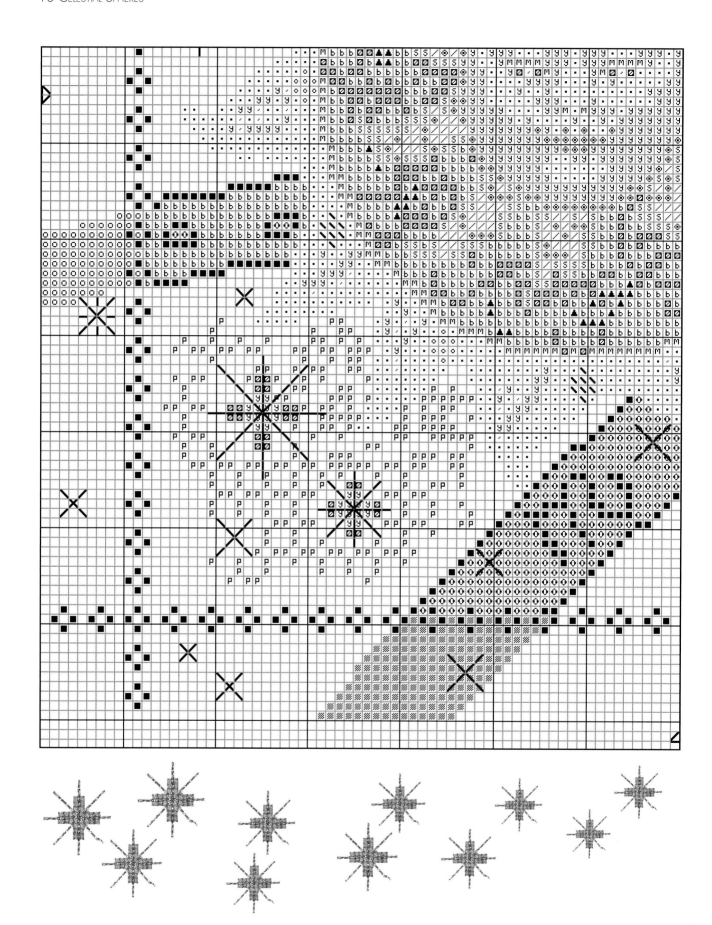

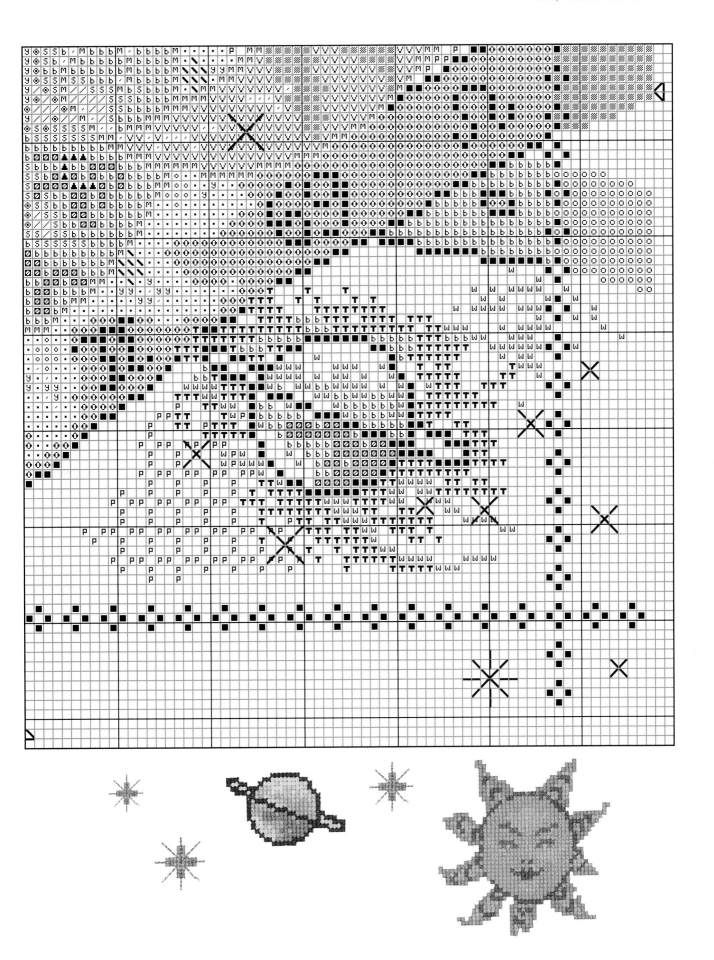

The Glory of the Sun

The moon, the sun and the stars look down on us unwaveringly from the heavens. During the day, the brightness and heat of the sun give us the light and warmth to live.

Design area (approx): 42 x 35cm (16½ x 13¾in) on 14 count ivory Aida or 27 count Linda.

Design size: 233 x 192 stitches. Allow for borders when cutting fabric.

STITCH AS FOLLOWS:
Use two strands of thread unless specified (S) = single strand. Backstitch is represented on the chart by a straight line (see Techniques, page 8).

1 Begin stitching at the centre and work outwards.

2 Complete the central area with backstitch, then build up the lettering.
BACKSTITCH COLOUR:
Sun motif (S) avocado green

3 Place the internal edge of the border and moons, followed by the corner blocks and the outer edge of the borders.

4 Work the border, then fill in the background.

5 Personalize with your own initials and date along dotted lines, using Alphabet 2 (see page 122) and honey brown.

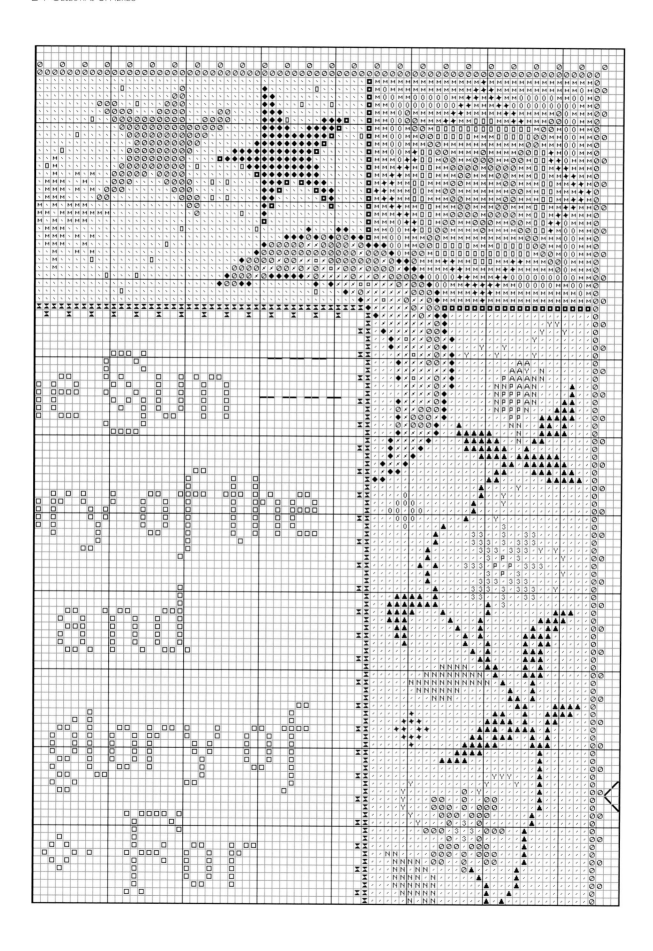

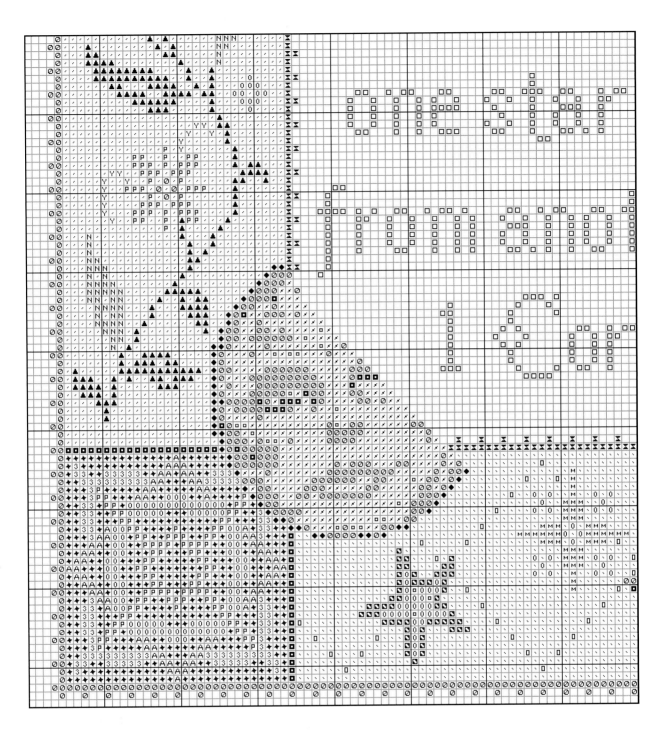

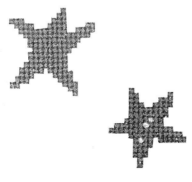

KEY TO CHART DIVISION

page 22	page 23	page 24
page 25	page 26	page 27

KEY

■	Indigo blue – deep	DMC 791
v	Blue mauve – very dark	DMC 333
◙	Blue mauve – medium	DMC 340
⊠	Blue mauve – light	DMC 341
♣	Purple	DMC 3746
▲	Avocado green	DMC 937
Ͷ	Yellow green	Anchor 280
◙	Bronze – light	DMC 833
.	Bronze – very light	DMC 834
◊	Golden brown – light	DMC 977
◪	Golden brown – medium	DMC 976
□	Honey brown	Anchor 369
ꓮ	Antique pink – light	DMC 3727
⌐	Lavender	DMC 211
ꓛ	Antique pink – dark	DMC 3726
3	Jade	DMC 992

Symbol	Colour	Code
✚	Peacock blue	DMC 3765
P	Dusty rose	DMC 3731
▯	Orange spice	DMC 720
2	Old gold – very light	DMC 677
Y	Sun gold	DMC 743
▯	White	
✓	Beige	Anchor 886

Child of the Universe

This timeless extract from the famous 'Desiderata' poem stands alone, and bears witness to our part in the great scheme of things. The text is often used on posters, and would make a great greetings card in cross stitch.

Design area (approx): 7 x 9cm (2¾ x 3½in) on18 count ivory Aida; 9 x 11cm (3½ x 4⅜in) on 14 count Aida; 12 x 15cm (4¾ x 6in) on 11 count Aida.

Design size: 45 x 62 stitches. Allow for borders when cutting fabric.

STITCH AS FOLLOWS:
On 18 count Aida use a single strand throughout the design; on 14 and 11 count Aida use two strands of thread. Backstitch is represented on the chart by a straight line (see Techniques, page 8).

1 Begin stitching at the centre and work outwards.

2 Add backstitch to the completed crosses.
BACKSTITCH COLOURS:
Text and leaf outlines Delft blue – light
Small motifs and hearts dusty pink – dark

3 To make the dot above the 'i', sew a stitch vertically over the hole by catching one strand of the fabric on either side .

4 Personalize with your own initials and date along the dotted lines, using Alphabet 4 (see page 123) and Delft blue – light.

KEY

⬡	Blue mauve	Anchor 118
⊡	Delft blue – light	DMC 809
◪	Purple	Anchor 119
✳	Dusty pink – dark	DMC 3687
⎕	Orange gold	Anchor 302
Я	Yellow bronze	DMC 733
◪	Antique green – dark	DMC 501
⊗	Antique green – medium	DMC 502
⬕	Antique green – light	DMC 503

When You Wish Upon a Star

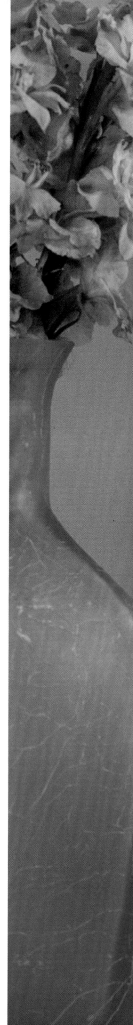

Hopes, dreams and aspirations are frequently associated with stars, and this song title, from the film Pinocchio, *is one of the most famous to express them. We make wishes, and we long for our dreams to come true.*

Design area (approx): 22 x 28cm (8¾ x 11in) on 14 count Aida or 27 count Linda.

Design size: 123 x 156 stitches. Allow for borders when cutting fabric.

STITCH AS FOLLOWS:

Use two strands of thread unless specified (S) = single strand. Backstitch is represented on the chart by a straight line (see Techniques, page 8).

1 Begin stitching at the centre and work outwards.

2 Add backstitch to the completed crosses.

BACKSTITCH COLOURS:

Sun face terracotta – strong
Text mix (S) blue grey and (S) indigo blue – deep
Stars same colour as star
Spirals at top (S) indigo blue – deep
Birds' eyes (S) indigo blue – deep
Hearts and spirals on drapes (S) metallic gold (see below)
Scrolls at top of columns indigo blue – deep
Columns (S) damson

3 Personalize with your own initials and date, using Alphabet 2 (see page 122).

USING METALLIC THREAD

Take one strand of thread and fold it in half. Thread the fold through the needle and then pass the needle through this loop and tighten; you now have enough thread attached to the needle to avoid slipping. Work a little more slowly to ensure that the thread sits neatly without looping.

When you wish
upon a ✳ Star it
makes no difference
who you are,
When you wish ✳
upon a ✳ Star
your dreams
come True

LFH   1995

KEY

⊡	Dusty rose – light	DMC 3354
✕	Dusty pink – medium	DMC 3687
✚	Damson	Anchor 872
■	Indigo blue – deep	DMC 791
⊕	Blue grey	Anchor 939
◇	Delft blue – very light	DMC 800
╱	White	
✛	Metallic gold	
▣	Terracotta – strong	Anchor 339
⊟	Honey brown	Anchor 369

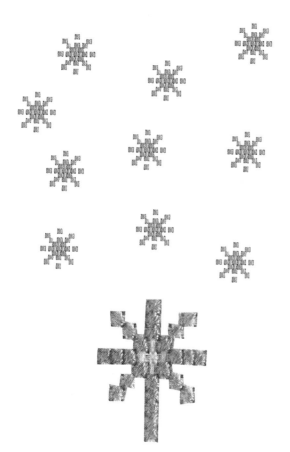

⊡	Soft orange	Anchor 1002
◇	Sun yellow	DMC 742
◪	Blue mix – one strand each of	
	indigo blue – deep	DMC 791
	and blue grey	Anchor 939

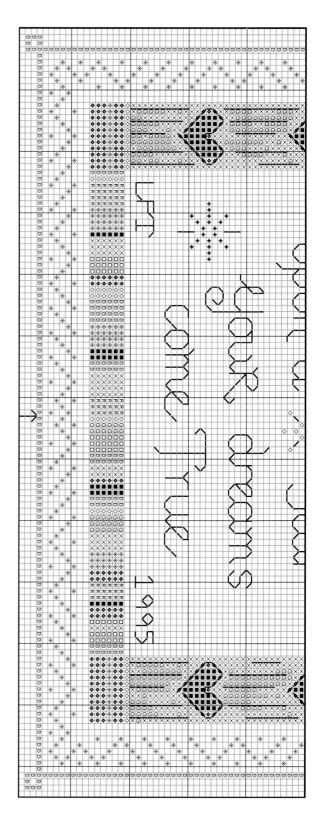

Sun Signs

The sun's energy gives us life, and the astrological signs associated with it influence our emotional journeys from life to death. This vibrant tableau is bordered by the twelve signs of the Zodiac.

Design area (approx): 22 x 22cm (8¾ x 8¾in) on 18 count navy Aida; 29 x 29cm (11½ x 11½in) on 14 count Aida.

Design size: 156 x 155 stitches. Allow for borders when cutting fabric.

Stitch as follows:
Use two strands of thread unless specified (S) = single thread. Backstitch is represented on the chart by a straight line (see Techniques, page 8).

1 Begin stitching at the centre and work outwards.

2 Place the borders.

3 Work the backstitch.
Backstitch colour:
All (S) blue violet – light.

4 Personalize with your own initials and date at bottom right of border, using Alphabet 2 (see page 122).

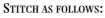

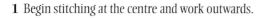

PISCES ♓ ARIES ♈ TAURUS ♉

GEMINI ♊

CANCER ♋

LEO ♌

LIBRA ♎ VIRGO ♍ LFH 1994 ♏

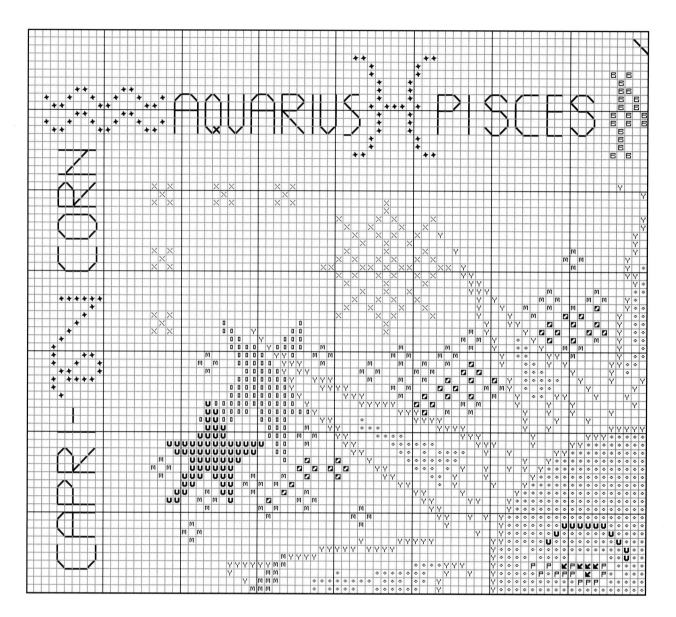

Key to chart division

page 36	page 37
page 38	page 39

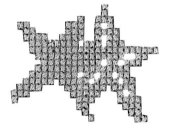

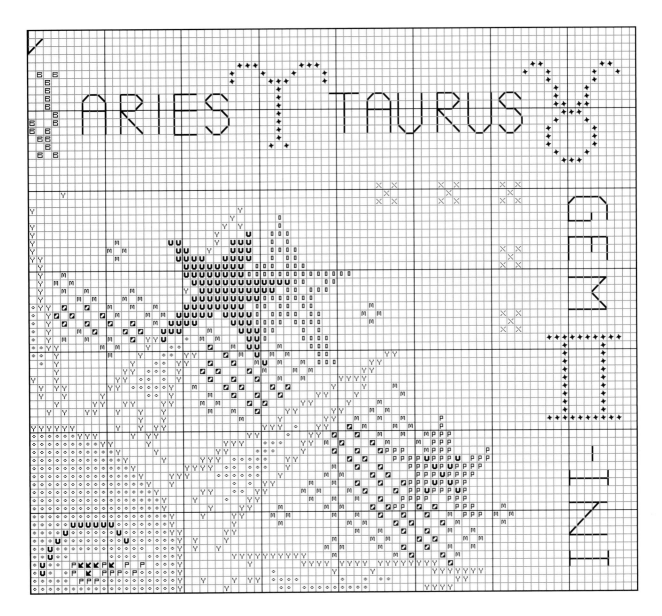

KEY

Symbol	Colour	Code
Y	Gold	Anchor 306
◦	Old gold	DMC 677
✦	Coral	DMC 351
P	Dusty rose – medium	DMC 3731
U	Dusty rose – light	DMC 3354
▯	Turquoise – light	DMC 598
⌺	Delft blue	DMC 809
M	Blue violet – light	DMC 341
◪	Blue violet – medium	DMC 340
✕	White	
◤	Black	DMC 310

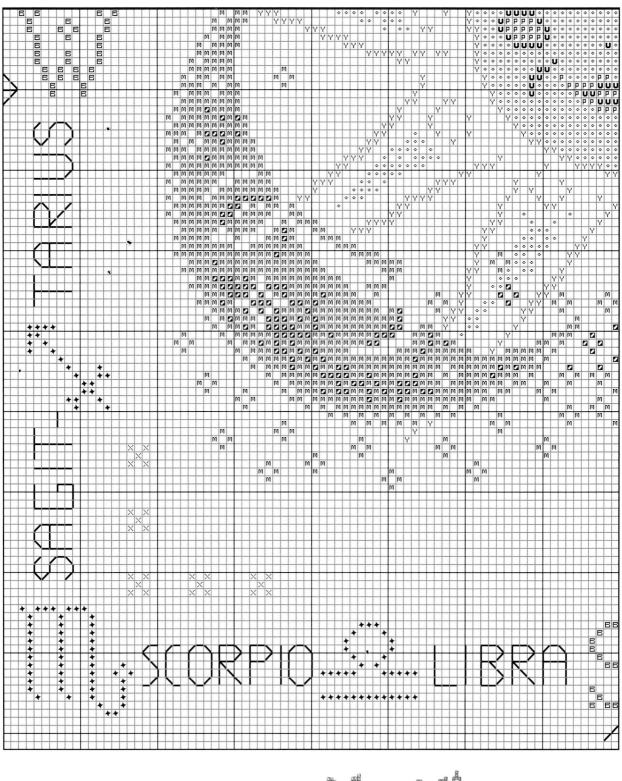

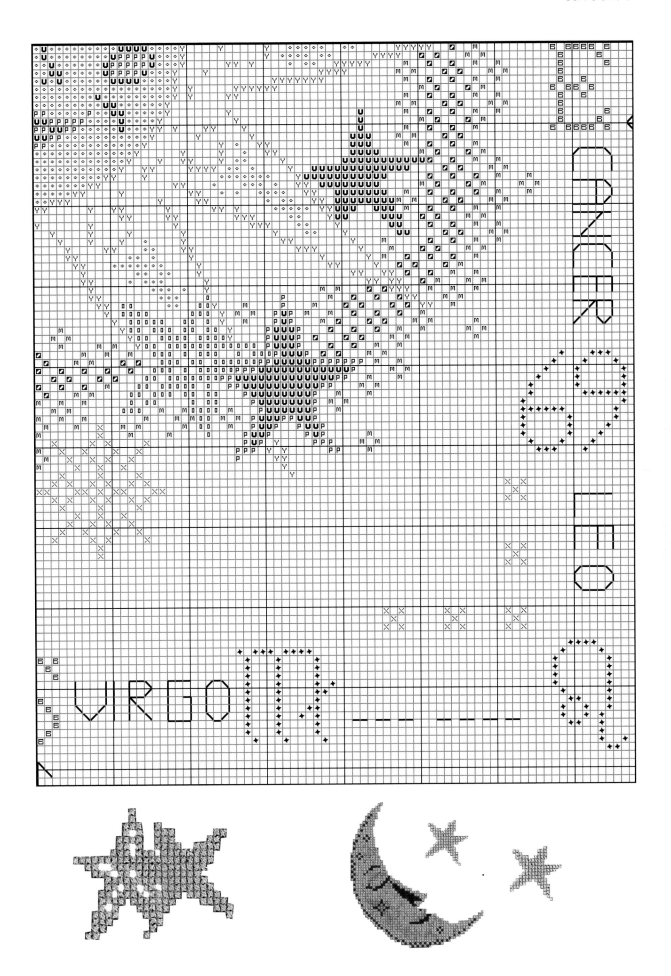

Myriad of Stars

*As well as being symbols of hopes and dreams and of the
unattainable, stars have for many centuries been
a means of navigation across the Earth.*

Design area (approx): 20 x 20cm (8 x 8in) on 14 count black Aida.

Design size: 107 x 108 stitches. Allow for borders when cutting fabric.

STITCH AS FOLLOWS:
Use two strands of thread throughout. Backstitch is represented on the
chart by a straight line (see Techniques, page 8).

1 Begin stitching at the centre and work outwards.

2 Add backstitch.
BACKSTITCH COLOURS:
Centre diamond mauve – light
Compass needle coral red
Lines between compass points white
Star names cornflower blue
Lower left stars in group aquamarine
Upper right stars in group mauve – light

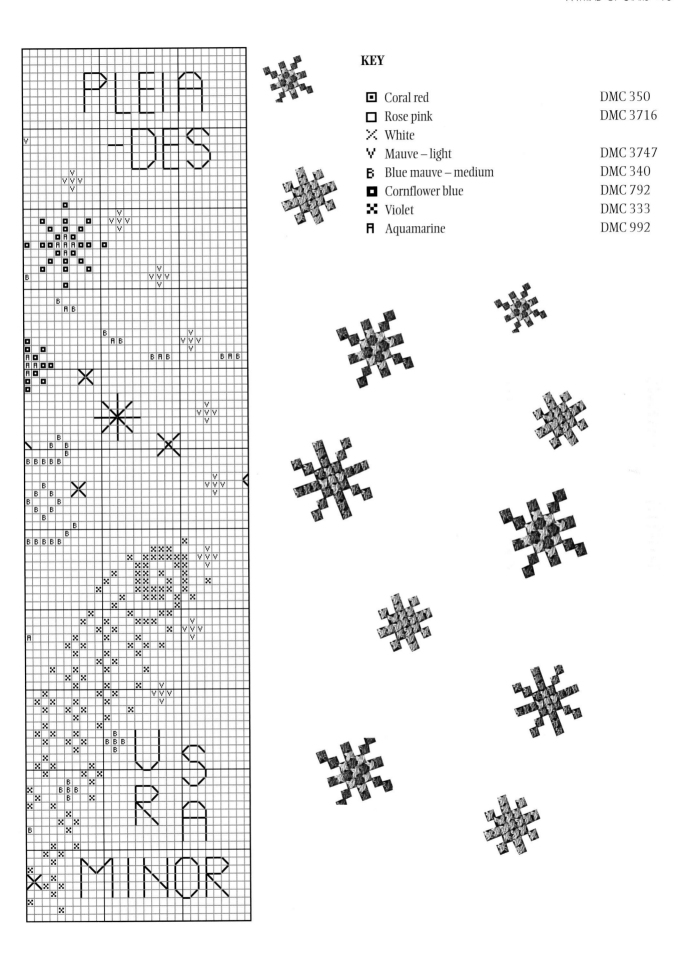

KEY

⊡	Coral red	DMC 350
☐	Rose pink	DMC 3716
✕	White	
V	Mauve – light	DMC 3747
B	Blue mauve – medium	DMC 340
⊡	Cornflower blue	DMC 792
✖	Violet	DMC 333
A	Aquamarine	DMC 992

HOUSE AND HOME

Samplers have traditionally featured the dual themes of house and home, and many fine examples are to be found in museums. The topics are perenially popular when stitchers wish to apply the fruits of their labour to decorate their homes. Our home is our personal creation, full of our treasures, our memories and our loved ones – both two- and four-legged varieties.

Favourite Things

This sampler features some of the delights and homely pleasures of life within a delicate patchwork design, with the words of the song from The Sound of Music *running around the border.*

Design area (approx): 24 x 24cm (9½ x 9½in) on 14 count ivory Aida or 27 count Linda; 22 x 22cm (8¾ x 8¾in) on 16 count Aida.

Design size: 138 x 138 stitches. Allow for borders when cutting fabric.

STITCH AS FOLLOWS:
Two strands are used unless marked (S) = single strand. Backstitch is represented on the chart by a straight line (see Techniques, page 8).

1 Begin stitching the heart motif at the centre and work outwards.

2 Build blocks around the heart. Complete the ginger squares at the intersections with rose – dark backstitch.

3 Work the picture blocks, colouring the backstitch.

BACKSTITCH COLOURS:
Dog: tail, chest same colour as body
    ears, hind leg ginger
    nose and mouth (S) indigo blue – dark
Flowers: stems oregano green
    bowl purple
Cat: tail, back, chest, ears ginger
    cross in motif to left of cat rose – dark
    other (S) indigo blue – dark
(continued on page 48)

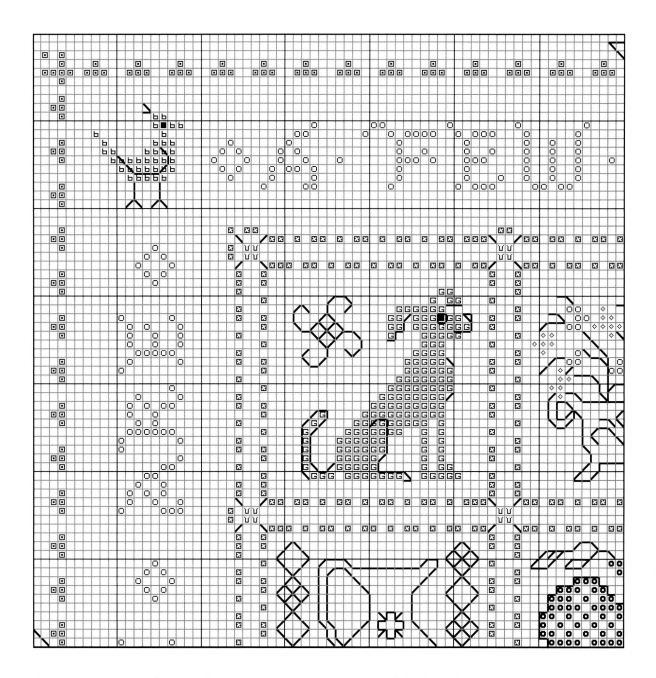

BACKSTITCH COLOURS (continued):

Jug: body purple

    borders (S) indigo blue – dark, making dots within

      squares (see fish, below)

Heart: leaves oregano green

      other rose – dark

Fish: bubbles and diagonals on centre

    of body ginger

    other – (S) indigo blue – dark

    centre of eyes to make a dot, sew a stitch vertically

      over the hole by catching one strand of the fabric on

      either side of the hole

Bird: bird purple

    borders see jug above

Tree: square motifs (S) indigo blue – dark

Teddy: square motifs (S) indigo blue – dark

      other ginger

Birds at corners: dark blue birds jade

          crests indigo blue – dark

          light blue birds indigo blue – dark

4 Place the lettering around the border and the birds at the corners.

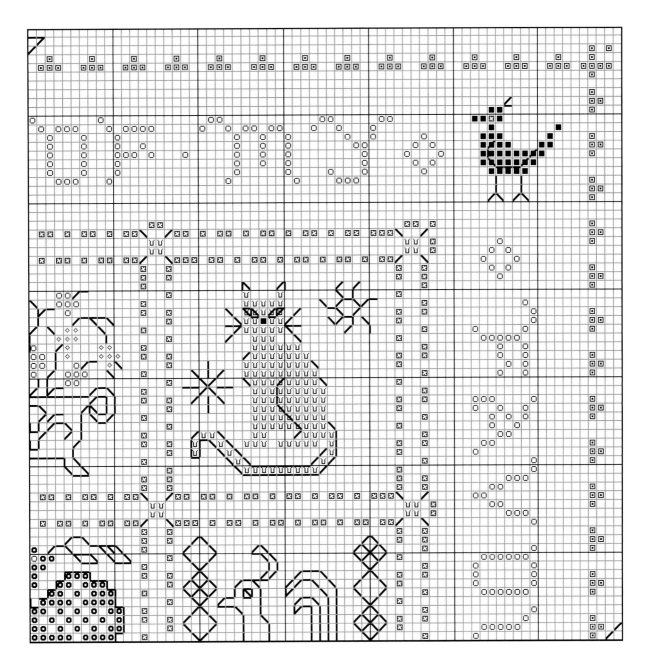

5 Place your own initials and date within the blocks along the bottom row, using Alphabet 5 (see page 124) and (S) indigo blue – dark. (If your initials do not fit into this space, remove the small diamonds.)

KEY

■	Indigo blue – dark	DMC 792
▣	Purple	DMC 3746
ᛕ	Indigo blue – light	DMC 794
⊠	Jade	DMC 992
⊘	Oregano green	DMC 3364
Ꮐ	Old gold	DMC 676
Ʊ	Ginger	Anchor 1001
▢	Rose – dark	DMC 309
◇	Dusty rose – light	DMC 3354
◎	Watermelon pink	DMC 760

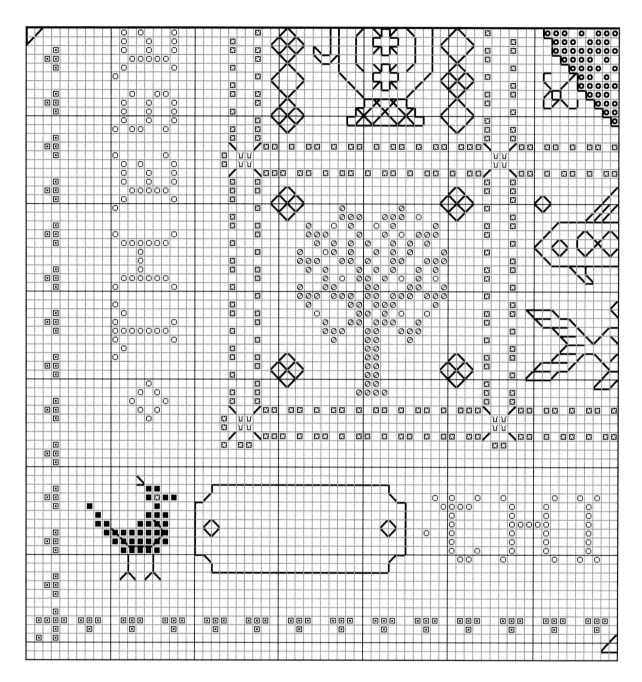

KEY TO CHART DIVISION

page 48	page 49
page 50	page 51

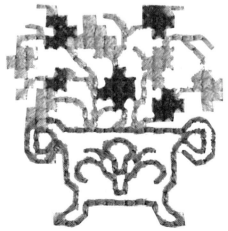

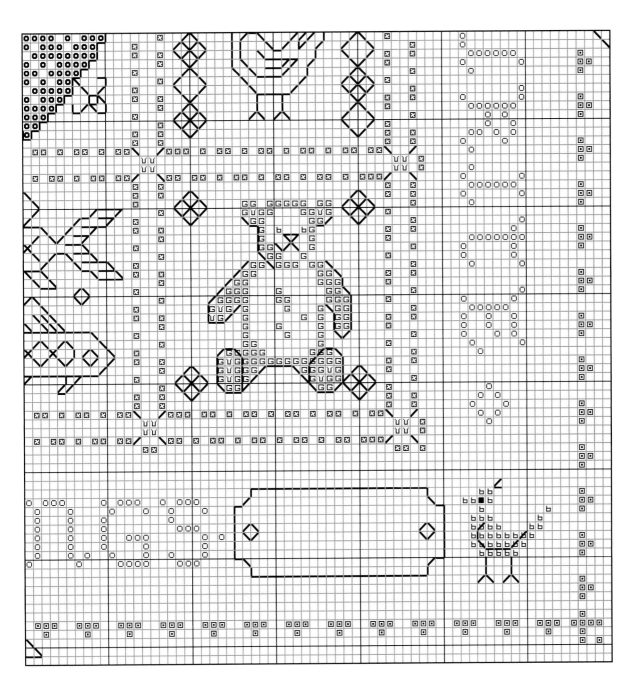

Bless This House

This simple sampler features a classic blessing, originally made popular in innumerable Victorian dwellings. It acts as a reminder to be thankful for the comfort, security and beauty of our home and its surroundings.

Design area (approx): 16 x 22cm (6¼ x 8¾in) on 16 count ivory Aida ; 19 x 26cm (7½ x 10¼in) on 14 count Aida

Design size: 139 x 100 stitches. Allow for borders when cutting fabric.

Stitch as follows:
Use two strands of thread. Backstitch is represented on the chart by a straight line (see Techniques, page 8).

1 Begin at the centre and work outwards. Place the borders.

2 Add the backstitch to the completed crosses; these stitches can be worked over two squares to get a more fluid line (see Techniques, page 8).

Backstitch colours:
Door and squiggles in bottom row chalk grey – dark
All other linen – dark

3 Select letters from Alphabet 6 (see page 125) to place your own initials within the box in the lower border of the design.

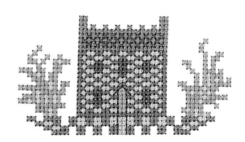

KEY

◨	Chalk grey – dark	DMC 645
▣	Linen – dark	DMC 642
Z	Tropical yellow-green	DMC 906
◇	Lettuce green	DMC 3348
◠	Old gold – light	DMC 676
G	Gold	DMC 725
✿	Gold – dark	DMC 783
⊟	Brick pink – medium	DMC 3778
○	Dusty rose – dark	DMC 3731
P	Watermelon pink	DMC 761
∕	Off-white	DMC 746

Home Sweet Home

This perennially favourite saying features the bright sun, birds in flight, a flourishing garden and a sound roof overhead. This would make a good design for a greetings card.

Design area (approx): 7 x 9cm (2¾ x 3½in) on 18 count ivory Aida; 9 x 11cm (3½ x 4⅜in) on 14 count Aida; 12 x 15cm (4¾ x 6in) on 11 count Aida.

Design size: 63 x 49 stitches. Allow for borders when cutting fabric.

STITCH AS FOLLOWS:

On 18 count Aida use a single strand throughout the design; on 14 and 11 count Aida use two strands of thread. Backstitch is represented on the chart by a straight line (see Techniques, page 8).

1 Begin stitching at the centre and work outwards.

2 Add backstitch to the completed crosses.

BACKSTITCH COLOURS:

Text dusty pink
Flowers below house green – dark
Design between flowers turquoise

3 Personalize with your own initials and date along dotted line, using Alphabet 4 (see page 123) and brick pink.

KEY

✦	Antique blue	Anchor 922
H	Brick pink	DMC 3778
५	Warm yellow	Anchor 302
▨	Dusty pink	DMC 3688
B	Blue mauve	Anchor 118
L	Lavender	DMC 209
◇	Turquoise	DMC 598
Z	Green – medium	Anchor 208
◪	Green – dark	DMC 501

LFH 1994

Home Sweet Home

Cat's Home

A wise feline knows how to satisfy its creature comforts, knows where to find its food – and occasionally deigns to honour us with its presence in the most comfortable place in the house.

Design area (approx): 18.5 x 12.5cm (7¼ x 5in) on 14 count ivory Aida.

Design size: 112 x 74 stitches. Allow for borders when cutting fabric.

STITCH AS FOLLOWS:

Two strands are used throughout unless marked (S) = single strand. Backstitch is represented on the chart by a straight line (see Techniques, page 8).

1 Begin stitching at the centre and work outwards.

2 Work the backstitch around the completed crosses.

BACKSTITCH COLOURS:

Wallpaper and floor line (S) yellow bronze
Flower bowl and window panes (S) navy blue/black
Curtains: top antique green
        bottom and window sill (S) antique green
Lettering dusty rose
Motifs on mat and at either side navy blue/black
Cat: eyes, nose, outline, whiskers outside head
  navy blue/black
    rest of body and whiskers (S) blue mauve – light

3 Stitch the lettering, then use blue mauve – light to oversew the dusty rose crosses on the curtains with a second cross.

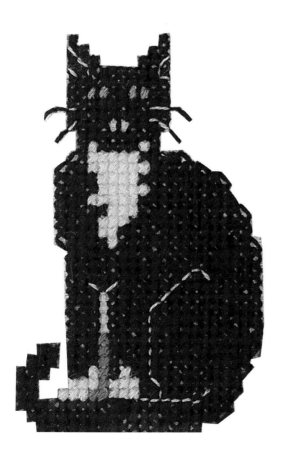

KEY

⌂	Delft blue – medium	DMC 798
◇	Navy blue/black	DMC 939
✚	Indigo blue	DMC 792
M	Blue mauve – light	DMC 341

▪	Sportsman flesh	DMC 3774
⁖	White	
⊠	Antique green	DMC 502
Z	Yellow bronze	DMC 733
Y	Yellow beige – light	DMC 3047
B	Dusty rose	DMC 3731

Helen B. Merry

This humorous saying from the nineteenth century provides us with a delightful motto for life. The gentle colours are reminiscent of a time when children were encouraged to learn stitching through making samplers.

Design area (approx): 22 x 16.5cm (8¾ x 6½in) on 14 count ivory Aida.

Design size: 123 x 87 stitches. Allow for borders when cutting fabric.

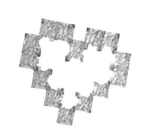

STITCH AS FOLLOWS:
Use two strands of thread. Backstitch is represented on the chart by a straight line (see Techniques, page 8).

1 Begin at the centre and work outwards.

2 Personalize with your own initials and date in the space marked by dotted lines, using Alphabet 3 (see page 123) and changing colours in the same way as for the other letters.

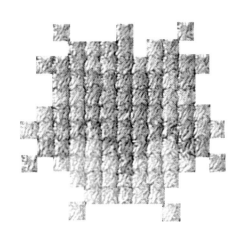

KEY

Z	Light copper	DMC 402
G	Old gold	DMC 676
□	Light tan	DMC 738
✕	Avocado green – light	DMC 471

△	Green grey	DMC 3023
□	Steel green	DMC 926
B	Sky blue	DMC 827
✧	Baby blue	DMC 775
◨	1 strand each	DMC 827 and 926

A Tidy House

A classic presentation of a contemporary saying: one to encourage us to sift out the important things in the midst of our over-busy lives, and to gladden the hearts of stitchers and creative people everywhere.

Design area (approx): 23 x 19cm (9 x 7½in) on 14 count ivory Aida or 27 count Linda.

Design size: 233 x 192 stitches. Allow for borders when cutting fabric.

STITCH AS FOLLOWS:
Use two strands of thread. Backstitch is represented on the chart by a straight line (see Techniques, page 8).

1 Begin at the centre and work outwards. Place the borders.

2 Work the backstitch over two squares to get a more fluid line (see Techniques, page 8).
BACKSTITCH COLOUR:
All ocean blue – medium

3 Personalize with your own initials and date, using Alphabet 1 (see page 122).

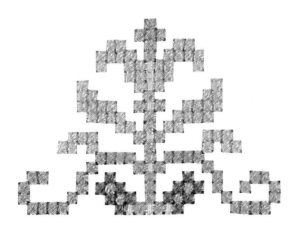

KEY

■	Antique blue – dark	DMC 931
ᴮ	Ocean blue – medium	DMC 519
◇	Sky blue tint	DMC 828
✖	Fresco green	DMC 3813
▪	Antique pink	DMC 224
╱	Antique red – light	DMC 223
ᴿ	Antique red – dark	DMC 3721

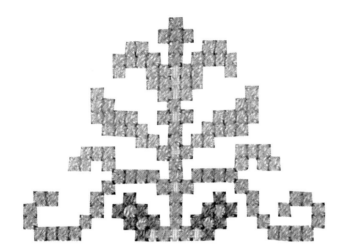

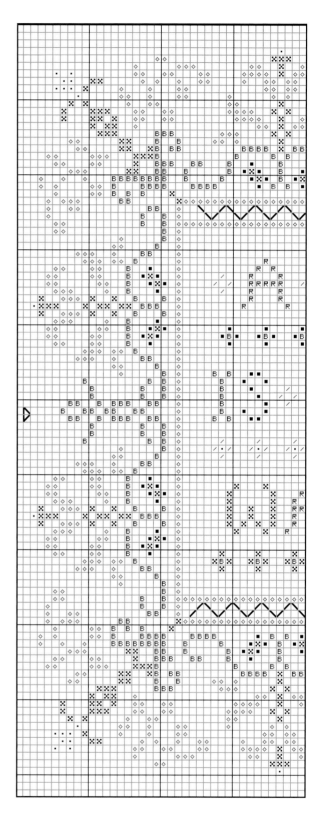

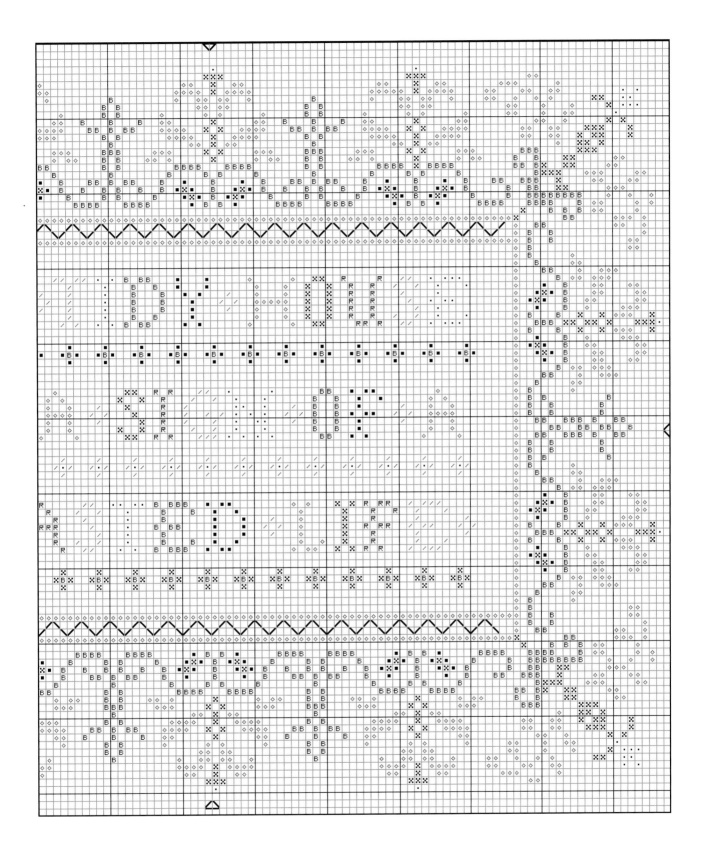

Nature

The natural world is full of miracles, and it is a source of endless inspiration to mankind – whether in a rough state, such as raw, open moorland and mountains, or a refined state, like the delicate petals of a flower. Nature is comprehensive and omnipresent: it is our essence and our life blood, and we continue to admire, imitate and interpret its beauty.

Many Eyes

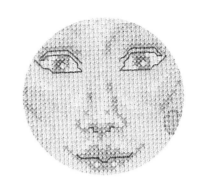

A timely quotation from Ralph Waldo Emerson, to remind us not to overlook the simple, nearby pleasures of life in our daily preoccupations. How could one pass over such a riot of flower colours?

Design area (approx): 28 x 32cm (11 x 12½in) on 14 count white Aida; 24 x 32cm (9½ x 12½in) on 16 count Aida.

Design size: 174 x 155 stitches. Allow for borders when cutting fabric.

STITCH AS FOLLOWS:
Use two strands of thread unless marked (S) = single strand. Backstitch is represented on the chart by a straight line (see Techniques, page 8).

1 Begin the lettering at the centre.

2 Build up the design around this.

3 Place the borders.

4 Add the backstitch to the completed crosses.
BACKSTITCH COLOURS:
(CLOCKWISE FROM FACE)
Eyes (S) blue mauve – dark
Lips, nostrils (S) antique red – dark
Chin (S) flesh – medium
Hair flesh – medium
Three blue flowers Delft blue – light
Pink flower to right of face (centre) watermelon pink – medium
Outer edge watermelon pink – light
Next pink flower watermelon pink – medium
Two small mauve flowers blue mauve – medium
Two small blue flowers blue mauve – dark
Small pink flower watermelon pink – light
Two large mauve flowers blue mauve – medium
Large pink flower watermelon pink – light

(CLOCKWISE FROM CENTRE BOTTOM)
Small pink flower watermelon pink – medium

Two tiny pink flowers watermelon pink – light
Two mauve flowers bottom left blue mauve – dark
Light pink flower watermelon pink – light
Dark pink flower watermelon pink – medium
Small blue and two mauve flowers blue mauve – dark
Pink flower watermelon pink – medium
Small light blue flower Delft blue – light
All pink flowers left of face watermelon pink – light
Small blue flower left of face Delft blue – light
All leaves olive green – medium
Outer border and initials Delft blue – light

5 Personalize with your own initials and date along dotted lines, using Alphabet 3 (see page 123).

Many eyes
Go through
the Meadow,
But few see
the Flowers

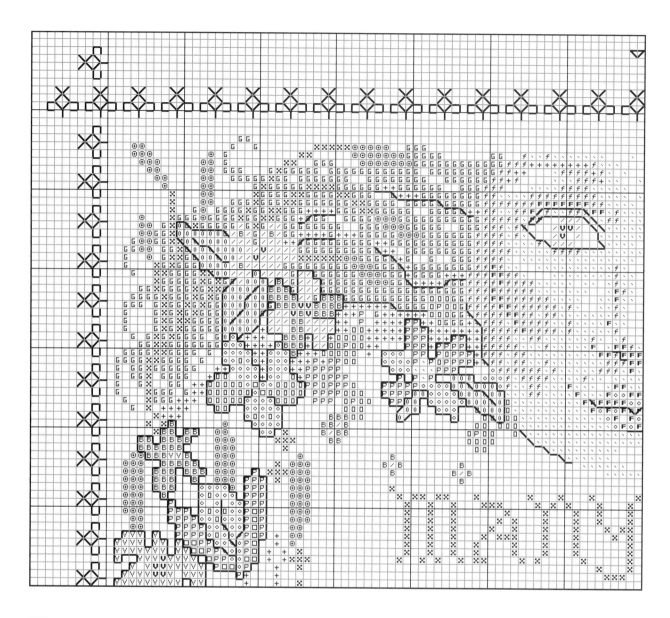

KEY

♣	Antique red – dark	DMC 3721
☐	Watermelon pink – medium	DMC 3328
P	Watermelon pink – light	DMC 760
○	Baby pink – medium	DMC 3326
▫	Watermelon pink – tint	DMC 3713
✖	Copper – very light	DMC 402
+	Old gold – light	DMC 676
G	Old gold – very light	DMC 677
▣	Bronze – light	DMC 833
⊘	Olive green – medium	DMC 3012
∴	Flesh – very light	DMC 3770
f	Flesh – light	DMC 3774
F	Flesh – medium	DMC 3773
⋃	Blue mauve – dark	DMC 3746
V	Blue mauve – medium	DMC 340
○	Blue mauve – very light	DMC 3747
╱	Delft blue – light	DMC 809
ℬ	Delft blue – very light	DMC 800
♭	Baby blue – very light	DMC 775
◊	Avocado green – very light	DMC 472

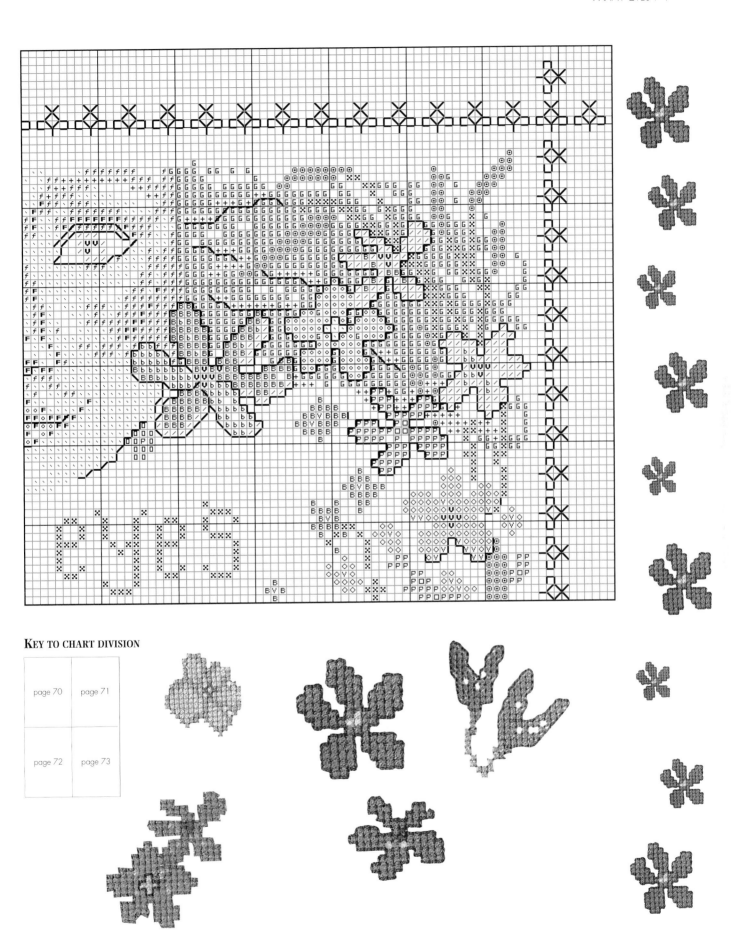

KEY TO CHART DIVISION

page 70	page 71
page 72	page 73

Blow the Wind

'Blow the wind southerly, southerly, southerly, Blow the wind south o'er the bonny blue sea...' This classic song encapsulates our wishes for nature to help our loved ones arrive safely at their destinations.

Design area (approx): 13 x 13cm (5⅛ x 5⅛in) on 16 count blue-grey (Zweigart 718) Aida; 15 x 15cm (6 x 6in) on 14 count Aida.

Design size: 85 x 85 stitches. Allow for borders when cutting fabric.

Stitch as follows:
Use two strands of thread, unless marked (S) = single strand. Backstitch is represented on the chart by a straight line (see Techniques, page 8).

1 Begin stitching at the centre and work outwards.

2 Add backstitch to the completed crosses.
Backstitch colours:
Eyes (S) indigo blue – deep
Face (except lips) (S) skin – dark
Lips and hair (S) russet
Edge of N/S/E/W blocks russet
Text and outer border (S) indigo blue – deep

3 Personalize with your own initials and date along the dotted lines, using Alphabet 1 (see page 122) and indigo blue – deep.

KEY

▣	Indigo blue – deep	DMC 9792
ᖯ	Indigo blue – light	DMC 794
Ⅱ	Sky blue tint	DMC 828
↗	White	
▪	Flesh – light	DMC 3774
✦	Flesh	DMC 950
■	Skin – dark	DMC 3772
♣	Yellow bronze – medium	DMC 733
▨	Russet	DMC 3830
₀	Soft orange	Anchor 1003
◇	Old gold – light	DMC 676
✕	Orange spice – light	Anchor 1002
⊓	Watermelon pink – light	DMC 760

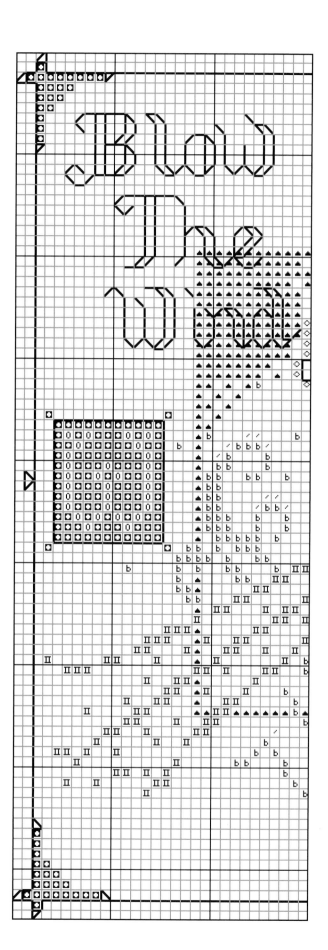

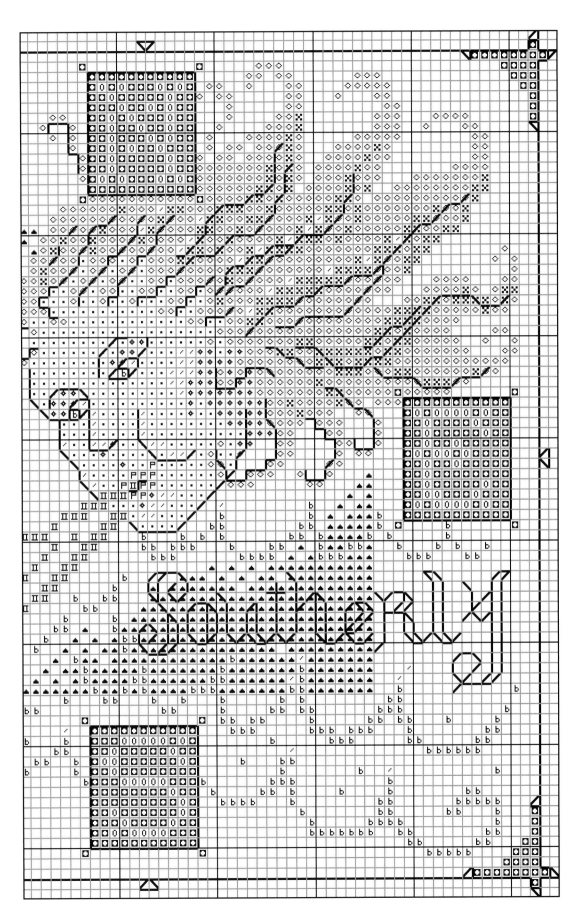

Olde Tree

This little tree bearing fruit is a timeless motif, found in paintings, tapestries and carvings alike. It is used here to commemorate a significant date – for instance, an anniversary or date of moving house.

Design area (approx): 3.5 x 5.3cm (1³⁄₈ x 2¹⁄₈ in) on18 count Aida; 4.5 x 6.5cm (1³⁄₄ x 2⁵⁄₈in) on 14 count Aida.

Design size: 36 x 23 stitches. Allow for borders when cutting fabric.

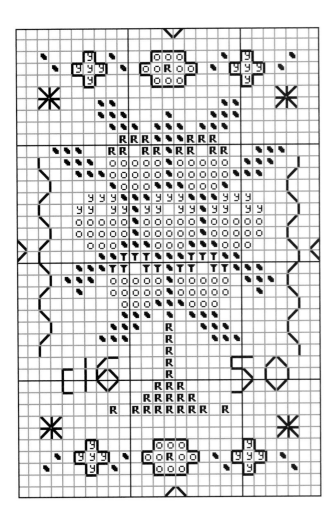

STITCH AS FOLLOWS:

On 18 count Aida use a single strand throughout the design. On 14 count Aida use two strands unless marked (S) = single strand. Backstitch is represented on the chart by a straight line (see Techniques, page 8).

1 Begin stitching at the centre and work outwards.

2 Add backstitch to the completed crosses.

BACKSTITCH COLOURS:

Flowers: top border (S) gold – pale
                bottom border (S) russet

Side border wavy lines russet

Running stitches tan

Squares: centres russet
                edges gold – dark

3 Personalize with a date as shown, using Alphabet 1 (see page 122) and green – dark.

KEY

ᴚ	Russet	DMC 3830
T	Tan	DMC 436
ש	Gold – dark	DMC 783
O	Gold – pale	DMC 676
❧	Green – dark	DMC 501

Poppies

Whether sparse in a hedgerow or covering a field on a hillside, the red poppy is a poignant and evocative symbol of summer. This floral spray, bordered with delicate lace, is in Victorian style.

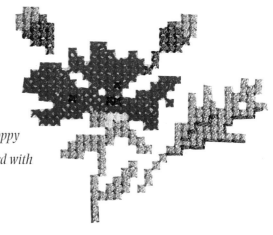

Design area (approx): 16 x 16cm (6¼ x 6¼in) on 14 count ivory Aida or 27 count Linda.

Design size: 91 x 92 stitches. Allow for borders when cutting fabric.

STITCH AS FOLLOWS:
Use two strands of thread. Backstitch is represented on the chart by a straight line (see Techniques, page 8).

1 Begin stitching at the centre and work outwards.

2 Place the borders carefully, ensuring they are symmetrical.

3 Work backstitch on the leaves.
BACKSTITCH COLOUR:
Leaves steel green – deep

KEY

✿	Old gold – dark	DMC 680
✕	Xmas red – bright	DMC 666
R	Xmas red – dark	DMC 321
▣	Lettuce green	DMC 3347
⋰	Steel green – medium	DMC 926
⌂	Steel green – light	DMC 927
☐	Steel green – deep	DMC 924
⬣	Jet black	DMC 310

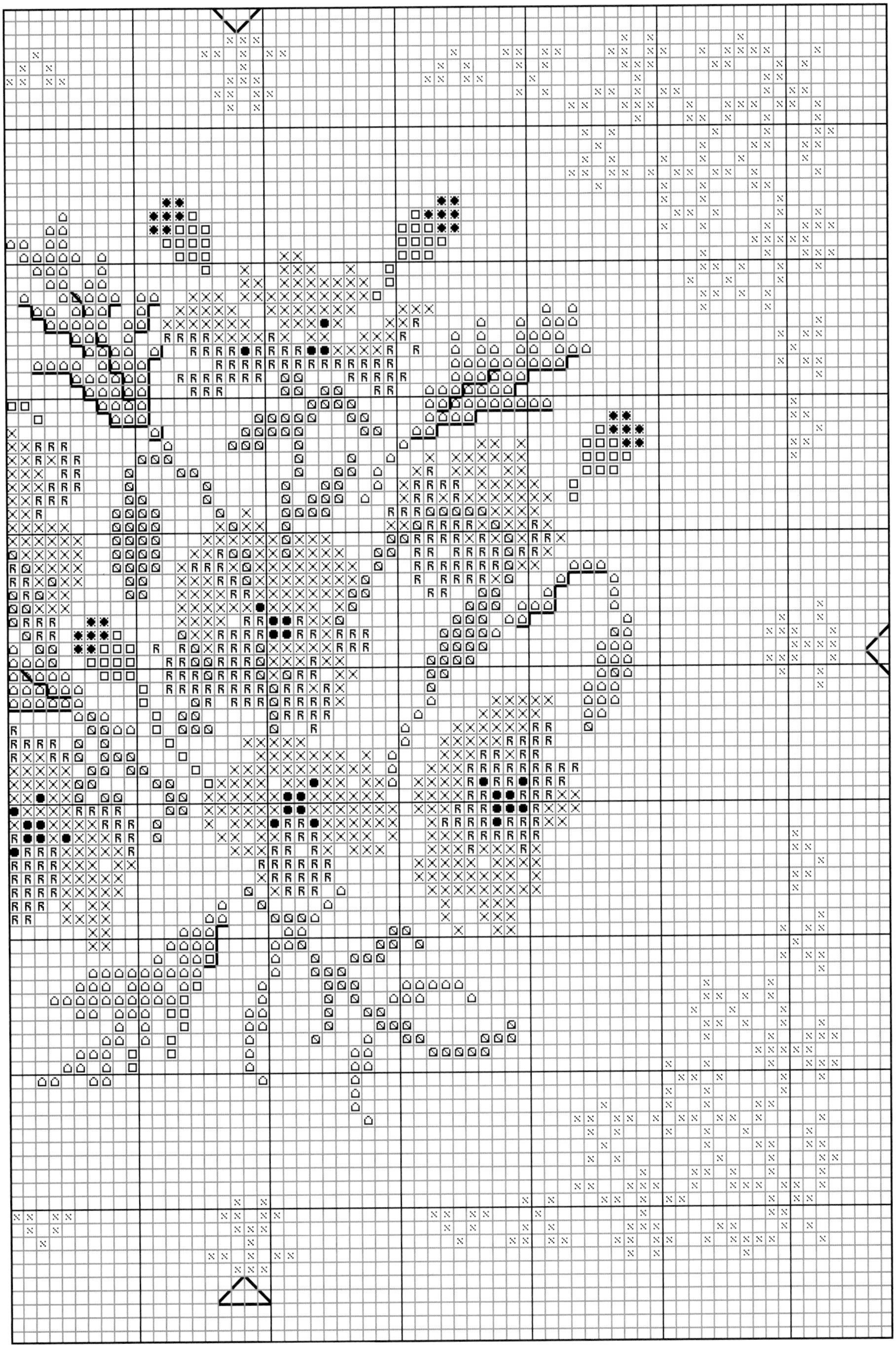

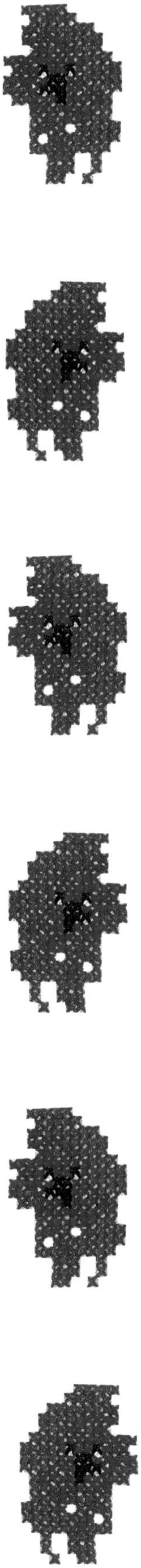

All Small Creatures

In the animal world the tail is an instrument of balance and status, a signal and a greeting, a flag and a symbol of pride – and we humans do not have one! This design would make a good greetings card.

Design area (approx): 7 x 9cm (2¾ x 3½in) on 18 count ivory Aida; 9 x 11cm (3½ x 4⅜in) on 14 count Aida; 12 x 15cm (4¾ x 6in) on 11 count Aida.

Design size: 66 x 51 stitches. Allow for borders when cutting fabric.

STITCH AS FOLLOWS:

On 18 count Aida use a single strand throughout; on 14 and 11 count Aida use two strands of thread, unless marked (S) = single strand. Backstitch is represented on the chart by a straight line (see Techniques, page 8).

1 Begin stitching at the centre and work outwards.

2 Add backstitch to the completed crosses.
BACKSTITCH COLOURS:
Text dusty rose – dark
Pink mice (S) terracotta – light
Other animals, leaves and bows same as cross stitch
Stems in side borders avocado green – light

3 Make French knots for eyes (see Techniques, page 8).

4 Personalize with your own initials and date along dotted line, using Alphabet 4 (see page 123) and terracotta – light.

KEY

❌	Dusty rose – dark	DMC 3731
⬕	Damson	Anchor 872
◇	Peacock blue	DMC 3766
⊠	Avocado green – light	DMC 471
H	Terracotta – light	Anchor 337
⌂	Pearl pink – very light	DMC 963
⅃	Soft gold	Anchor 311

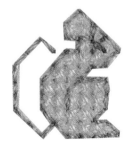

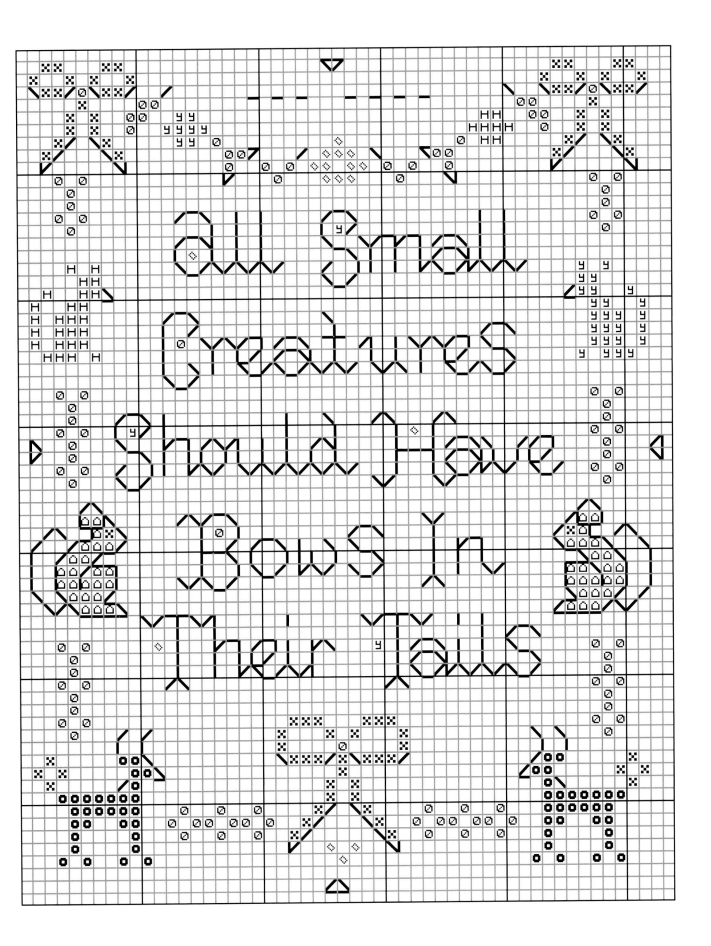

Bird of Love

The Bird of Love has been a powerful symbol of romance for hundreds of years.
This delightful sampler could be worked to commemorate a special moment, or
act as a memento of emotions recalled in tranquillity.

Design area (approx): 12.5 x 12.5cm (5 x 5in) on 14 count
ivory Aida or 27 count Linda.

Design size: 70 x 72 stitches. Allow for borders when
cutting fabric.

STITCH AS FOLLOWS:

Use two strands unless marked (S) = single strand.
Backstitch is represented on the chart by a straight line
(see Techniques, page 8).

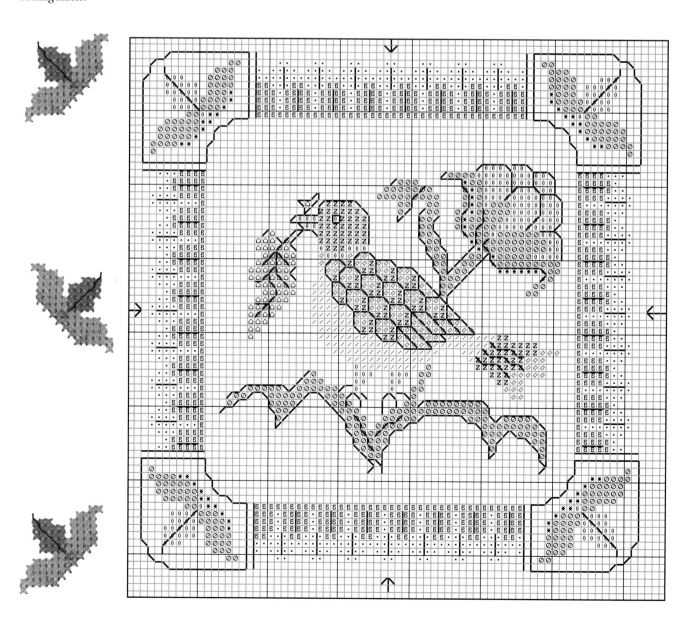

1 Begin stitching at the centre and work outwards

2 Add backstitch to the completed crosses.

BACKSTITCH COLOURS:

Borders (S) navy blue – dark

Bird: all feather detail (S) mauve

    outline head (not beak) (S) orange spice

    beak, eye, claws (S) navy blue – dark

Flower above bird: stems sap green

        green leaf detail (S) navy blue – dark

        orange flower head (S) mauve

Stalk below bird (S) mauve

KEY

■ Navy blue – dark		DMC 823
H Mauve		DMC 3746
E Blue mauve – medium		DMC 340
▪ Blue mauve – light		DMC 3747
⌂ Antique green		DMC 503
0 Orange spice		DMC 720
Z Sun gold		DMC 743
◇ Sun gold tint		DMC 745
Ø Yellow green		Anchor 280
✸ Sap green		Anchor 266
╱ Blue mauve mix – one strand each of		
	blue mauve – medium	DMC 340
	and blue mauve – light	DMC 3747

Harvest Mouse

As the high summer sun beats down upon fully laden sheaves of glowing golden corn, the acrobatic harvest mouse busies himself foraging for seeds, grain, soft fruit and insects.

Design area (approx): 16 x 16cm (6¼ x 6¼in) on 14 count Aida or 27 count Linda.

Design size: 91 x 92 stitches. Allow for borders when cutting fabric.

STITCH AS FOLLOWS:
Use two strands unless marked (S) = single strand. Backstitch is represented on the chart by a straight line (see Techniques, page 8).

1 Begin stitching at the centre and work outwards. Take care to place the borders evenly (continued on page 91).

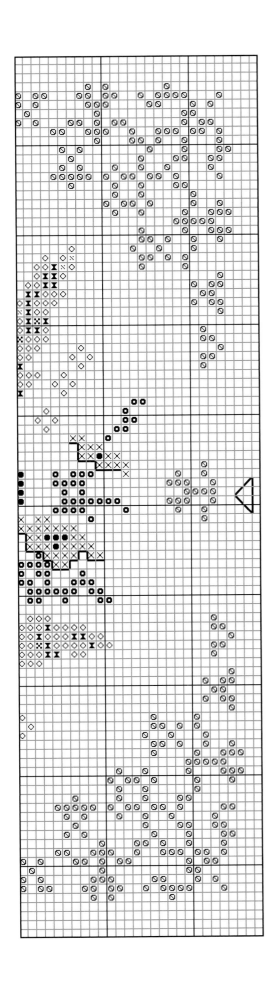

(continued from page 88)

2 Work backstitch on the mouse and flowers.

BACKSTITCH COLOURS:

Mouse (S) walnut brown

Flowers walnut brown

KEY

⁚⁚	Old gold – very light	DMC 677
◇	Old gold – light	DMC 676
□	Tan	DMC 436
●	Walnut brown	DMC 3781
⊥	Yellow bronze – light	DMC 734
◘	Antique green – light	DMC 503
⊘	Fresco green – light	DMC 3813
✕	Xmas red	DMC 666
℗	Peach	DMC 353
▪	White	
✖	Green mix – one strand each of	
	walnut brown	DMC 3781
	and yellow bronze – light	DMC 734

THE GARDEN

Gardens are sanctuaries where we can enjoy the freedom to express our pleasure in plants and landscapes – large and small. It is a place to be at ease with ourselves and to watch the interplay of nature and nurture, where light, air and water combine in the essence of creation. In this space we take time out to relax and rest, and to gain inspiration.

The Dovecote

The cooing of doves heralds the coming of spring and the return of life after the depths of winter. With its white birds darting in and out, this dovecote will be a reminder of this fresh season all the year round.

Design area (approx): 8.3 x 16cm (3¼ x 6¼in) on 14 count ivory or rustico Aida or 27 count Linda.

Design size: 93 x 45 stitches. Allow for borders when cutting fabric.

STITCH AS FOLLOWS:
Use two strands of thread unless marked (S) = single strand. Backstitch is represented on the chart by a straight line (see Techniques, page 8).

1 Begin stitching at the centre and work outwards. Place the borders.

2 Add backstitch after completing the crosses.
BACKSTITCH COLOURS:
Sides of roof and triangles on house (S) nutmeg
Details on windows deep green
Orange flowers (S) terracotta
Birds and white flowers deep green
Blue flowers baby blue tint
Bottom of roof and sides of house, triangles on roof, detail on wood, foliage and fence (S) deep green

3 As a finishing touch, purchase and attach a brass butterfly charm to one of the flowers.

KEY

▢	White	
·	Baby blue tint	DMC 3756
▵	Deep green	DMC 974
✖	Willow green	DMC 320
◈	Moss green	DMC 733
▪	Soft orange	Anchor 1002
ᴛ	Terracotta	DMC 920
■	Nutmeg	DMC 433

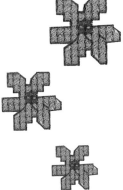

The Beehive

In this tribute to the bee and the summer months, you can almost smell honeysuckle mingling with the warmth of the sun. Among the flowers the bees diligently collect the harvest to deposit in the honeycombs inside their warm hives.

Design area (approx): 8.3 x 16cm (3¼ x 6¼ in) on 14 count Aida or 27 count Linda.

Design size: 93 x 49 stitches. Allow for borders when cutting fabric.

STITCH AS FOLLOWS:

Use two strands unless marked (S) = single strand. Backstitch is represented on the chart by a straight line (see Techniques, page 8).

1 Begin stitching at the centre and work outwards. Place the borders.

2 Add backstitch after completing the crosses.
BACKSTITCH COLOURS:
Large honeycomb bronze
Everything else (S) bronze

3 Using Alphabet 4 (see page 123), place your own initials along the dotted line with (S) bronze.

4 Purchase and attach a brass bee charm to the beehive.

KEY

⌂	Yellow beige – light	DMC 3047
G	Old gold – medium	DMC 729
8	Old gold – dark	DMC 680
■	Bronze	DMC 829
⊘	Avocado green – light	DMC 471
▢	Avocado green – medium	DMC 937
◇	Antique blue	DMC 3753
m	Blue mauve	DMC 340
V	Violet – very light	DMC 554

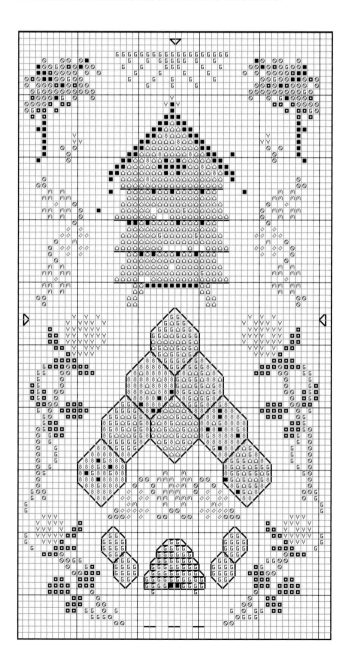

The Topiary Garden

Topiary gardens have been striking features in the great gardens of Europe since Roman times. The classic, architectural construction of clipped hedges and shrubs brings calmer, more ordered days to mind.

Design area (approx): 27 x 15cm (10½ x 6in) on 14 count ivory or rustico Aida or 27 count Linda.

Design size: 150 x 71 stitches. Allow for borders when cutting fabric.

STITCH AS FOLLOWS:
Use two strands unless marked (S) = single strand. Backstitch is represented on the chart by a straight line (see Techniques, page 8).

1 Begin stitching at the centre and work outwards. Place the borders.

2 Add backstitch after completing the crosses.
BACKSTITCH COLOURS:
Gate indigo blue – dark
Plant pots (S) indigo blue – dark
Birds' beaks and mazes (S) willow green
Trees: left side in both borders (S) indigo blue – dark
      right side in both borders yellow beige
Balustrade (S) moss green

3 Personalize with your own initials and one strand of each of indigo and willow. Using Alphabet 2 (see page 122), place your own initials and date along the dotted lines above the hedges.

KEY

Π	Navy blue – dark	DMC 823
♣	Indigo blue – dark	DMC 792
■	Willow green – very dark	DMC 319
+	(S) Willow	DMC 319
III	Moss green	DMC 581
∅	Tropical yellow green	DMC 906
◇	Antique olive	DMC 3012
◘	Terracotta – medium	DMC 920
T	Terracotta – light	DMC 922

Υ	Yellow beige	DMC 3046
▪	White	

✔ Indigo blue and willow mix – one strand each of

Indigo blue – dark	DMC 792
and Willow green – very dark	DMC 319

✕ Willow green and navy blue mix – one strand each of

Willow green – very dark	DMC 319
and navy blue – dark	DMC 823

Z Terracotta and yellow beige mix – one strand each of

Terracotta – light	DMC 922
and yellow beige	DMC 3046

A Flower Cannot Blossom

The eloquent proverb in this little sampler conjures up the natural forces of sun, rain, darkness and light, and the elements of creation, germination and growth. This would make a good greetings card.

Design area (approx): 7 x 9cm (2¾ x 3½in) on18 count ivory Aida; 9 x 11cm (3½ x 4⅜in) on 14 count Aida; 12 x 15cm (4¾ x 6in) on 11 count Aida.

Design size: 62 x 47 stitches. Allow for borders when cutting fabric.

STITCH AS FOLLOWS:
On 18 count Aida use a single strand throughout the design; on 14 and 11 count Aida use two strands of thread. Backstitch is represented on the chart by a straight line (see Techniques, page 8).

1 Begin the flower motif at the centre and work outwards. Place the borders.

2 Add backstitch to the completed crosses.
BACKSTITCH COLOURS:
Text antique blue – dark
Stems and motifs within borders green – dark

3 Personalize with your own initials and date along the dotted lines, using Alphabet 4 (see page 123) and antique blue – dark.

KEY

ᗷ	Blue grey	Anchor 939
ᗐ	Lilac	Anchor 108
ᗕ	Honey	Anchor 363
ᖴ	Terracotta – light	Anchor 337
ᑕ	Rose pink	DMC 335
ᔕ	Green – medium	Anchor 208
ᗅ	Green – dark	Anchor 877
ᗕ	Antique blue – dark	Anchor 922

A Topiary Bird

Deriving from the Latin word 'toparius', meaning gardener, topiary is the art of pruning and shaping evergreen shrubs to create fanciful shapes. Silhouettes are its defining features.

Design area (approx): 16 x 8cm (6¼ x 3⅛in) on 14 count Aida or 27 count Linda.

Design size: 123 x 156 stitches. Allow for borders when cutting fabric.

STITCH AS FOLLOWS:
Use two strands unless marked (S) = single strand. Backstitch is represented on the chart by a straight line (see Techniques, page 8).

1 Begin stitching at the centre and work outwards.

2 Place the borders. Add backstitch after completing the crosses.
BACKSTITCH COLOUR:
All willow green – dark

3 Attach a ladybird charm with (S) willow green – dark.

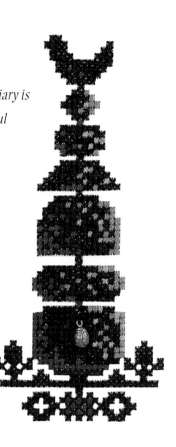

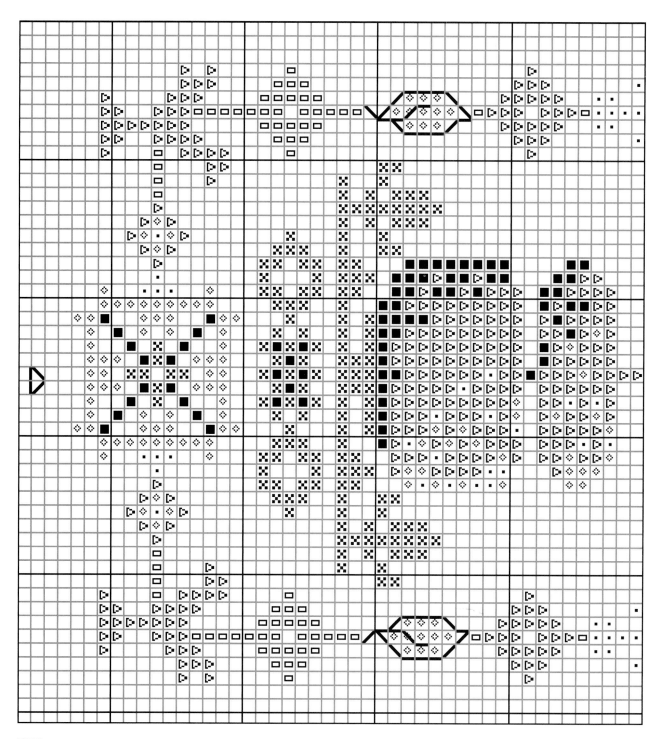

KEY

✕	Indigo blue – deep	DMC 791
■	Indigo blue	DMC 792
▲	Willow green – dark	DMC 319
◇	Moss green	DMC 581
▪	Old gold	DMC 729
▫	Terracotta	DMC 920

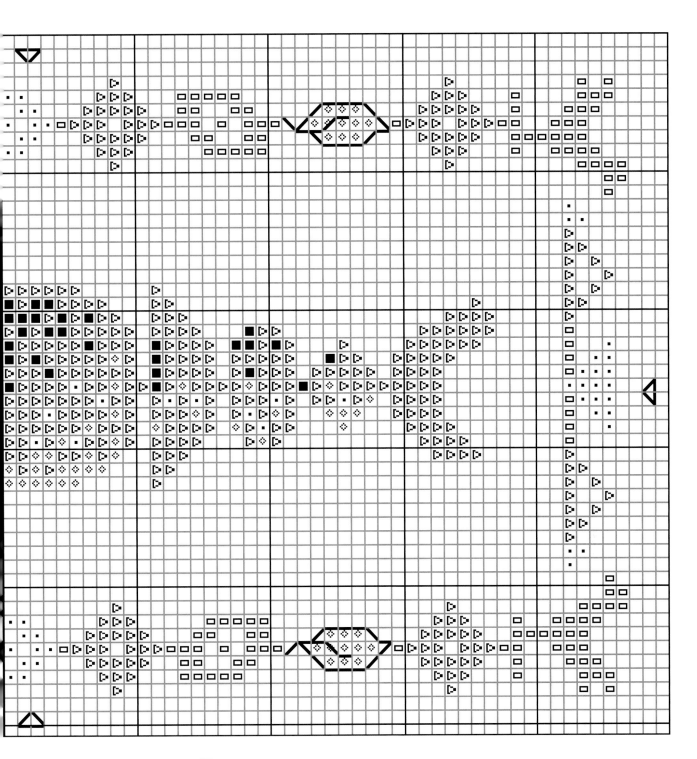

A B C D E

F G H I J

K L M N

O P Q R

R S T U

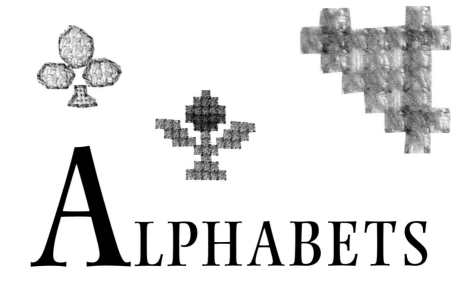

ALPHABETS

The word 'sampler' is derived from the Latin word *exemplum*, meaning an example. The original purpose of embroidered samplers was as a learning exercise for remembering and practising – and passing on to others – alphabets before the advent of mass printing. The alphabet makes a beautiful collection of graphic shapes which can be enjoyed in their own right, and as a vehicle for communication.

Cross Stitch Alphabet

The unique characteristics of a set of letters creates a pattern that is both simple and beautiful. Alphabet samplers were a staple of cross stitch in Victorian times and continue to make fascinating projects.

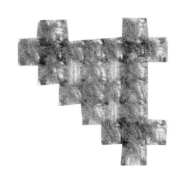

Design area (approx): 7 x 9cm (2¾ x 3½in) on 18 count ivory Aida; 9 x 11cm (3½ x 4⅜in) on 14 count Aida; 12 x 15cm (4¾ x 6in) on 11 count Aida.

Design size: 63 x 47 stitches. Allow for borders when cutting fabric.

STITCH AS FOLLOWS:

On 18 count Aida use a single strand throughout the design; on 14 and 11 count Aida use two strands of thread. Backstitch is represented on the chart by a straight line (see Techniques, page 8).

1 Begin stitching from the centre and and work outwards.

2 Add backstitch to the completed crosses.
BACKSTITCH COLOUR:
Crosses Delft blue – dark

3 Personalize with your own initials and date along the dotted line, using Alphabet 4 (see page 123) and Delft blue – dark.

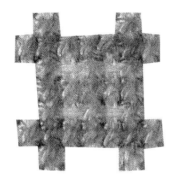

KEY

♣	Delft blue – dark	DMC 798
⊟	Blue mauve	Anchor 118
✿	Lavender	DMC 210
℞	Rose pink	DMC 335
◣	Turquoise	DMC 597
⊠	Green – medium	Anchor 208
◻	Yellow bronze	DMC 733
Y	Orange gold	Anchor 311
⊽	Brick pink – light	DMC 758
U	Brick pink – medium	DMC 3778

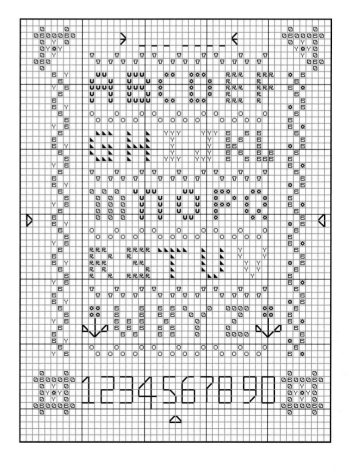

Backstitch Alphabet

Language and the written word pervade our culture and very existence. The alphabet stands alone as a vehicle of decoration in which scale and colour are used with endearing charm.

Design area (approx): 7 x 9cm (2¾ x 3½in) on18 count ivory Aida; 9 x 11cm (3½ x 4⅜in) on 14 count Aida; 12 x 15cm (4¾ x 6in) on 11 count Aida.

Design size: 60 x 47 stitches. Allow for borders when cutting fabric.

STITCH AS FOLLOWS:
On 18 count Aida use a single strand throughout the design; on 14 and 11 count Aida use two strands of thread. Backstitch is represented on the chart by a straight line (see Techniques, page 8).

1 Begin stitching at the centre and work outwards.

2 Add backstitch to the completed crosses.
BACKSTITCH COLOURS:
Main grid light brown
Lettering within grid topaz
ABC bottom row russet

3 Personalize with your own initials and date along dotted line, using Alphabet 4 (see page 123) and russet.

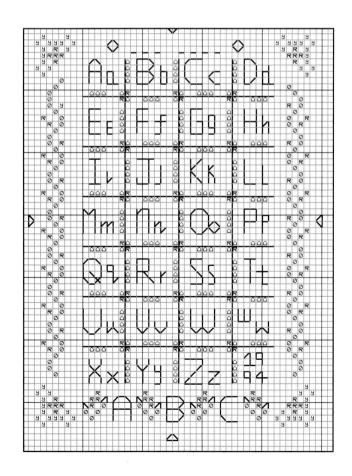

KEY

⊘	Steel green	DMC 926
Y	Topaz	DMC 782
⌂	Light brown	DMC 613
R	Russet	DMC 3830

Harvest Alphabet

This alphabet sampler celebrates a special time of year in the country calendar: ripe fruits are piled high, grain is stored in the barn, acorns are falling, and it is time to pause and give thanks for the yield.

Design area (approx): 30 x 23cm (12 x 9in) on 14 count ivory Aida or 27 count Linda.

Design size: 158 x 119 stitches. Allow for borders when cutting fabric.

STITCH AS FOLLOWS:
Use two strands of thread. Backstitch is represented on the chart by a straight line (see Techniques, page 8).

1 Begin stitching at the centre and work outwards.

2 Add backstitch to the completed cross stitch.
BACKSTITCH COLOURS:
House windows sky blue tint
Four corners antique red – dark

3 Add French knots (see Techniques, page 8) to all terracotta triangles in the border. On the diagram below left, the black dots represent the knots.

POSITION OF FRENCH KNOTS

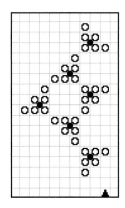

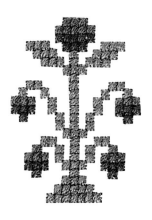

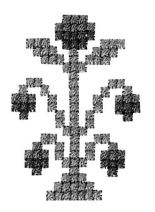

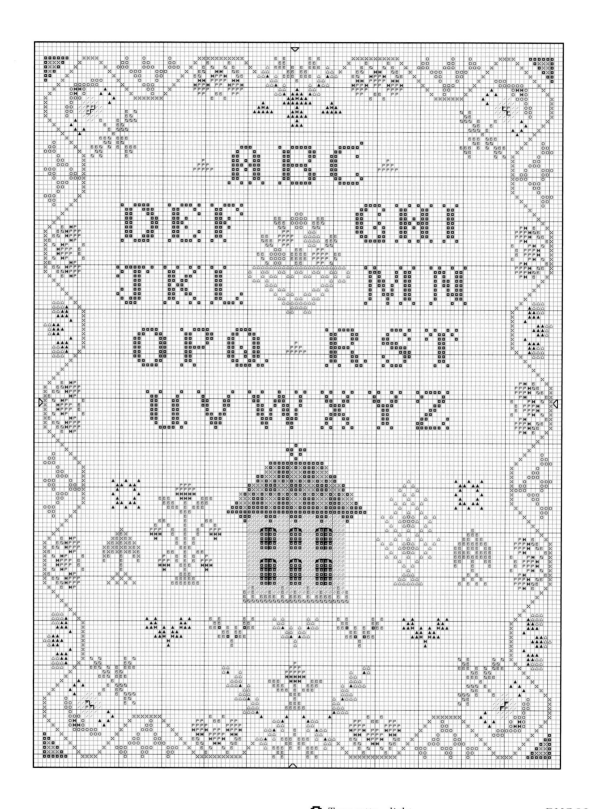

KEY

◼ Prussian blue	DMC 312	
✖ Ocean blue	DMC 518	
◈ Sky blue tint	DMC 828	
◙ Antique green	DMC 502	
Ɛ Avocado green	DMC 470	

◖ Terracotta – light	DMC 922
▲ Warm brown – very light	DMC 435
Ᵽ Coral pink	DMC 351
⟋ Brick pink – light	DMC 758
H Antique red – dark	DMC 3721
⌂ Old gold	DMC 729

White Alphabet

The written word in its many forms can be enjoyed in the form of a classical alphabet with a calligraphic style. The relief decoration is white on white and light on light, using natural cotton and linen.

Design area (approx): 20 x 29cm (8 x 11½in) on 14 count Aida or 27 count Linda.

Design size: 110 x 161 stitches. Allow for borders when cutting fabric.

STITCH AS FOLLOWS:

1 Begin stitching at the centre and work outwards.

2 Work the four large eyelets beside the 'O' and 'Q'(see below), then work a smaller version over the square area between them.

3 Work the fan motifs (see below).

4 On the fans, create one large cross stitch by working two half stitches on top of each other in one direction, then cover these with two half stitches in the other direction.

5 For the flower motifs use natural pearl cotton, working one long stitch over a full length of backstitch. For the zigzags at the bottom, use natural pearl cotton and long stitch. Sew from left to right so that stitches are interwoven, i.e. over at one end and under at the other end.

STITCHING THE EYELETS:
Each motif consists of four eyelets with a small eyelet at the centre. Using white pearl cotton, bring the thread up at odd numbers and down at the centre 'eye'. Work around until the circle is complete, keeping the thread fairly taut. On Aida work over two squares – sew only the alternate stitches illustrated and do not stitch into the centre of a square.

STITCHING THE FANS:
Each fan (indicated on the chart by a right angle in backstitch) consists of four fans at various angles with a large cross stitch at the centre. Using natural pearl cotton, bring the thread up at odd numbers and down at the centre. Work around until the right angle is complete, keeping the thread fairly taut so that the eye remains passable.

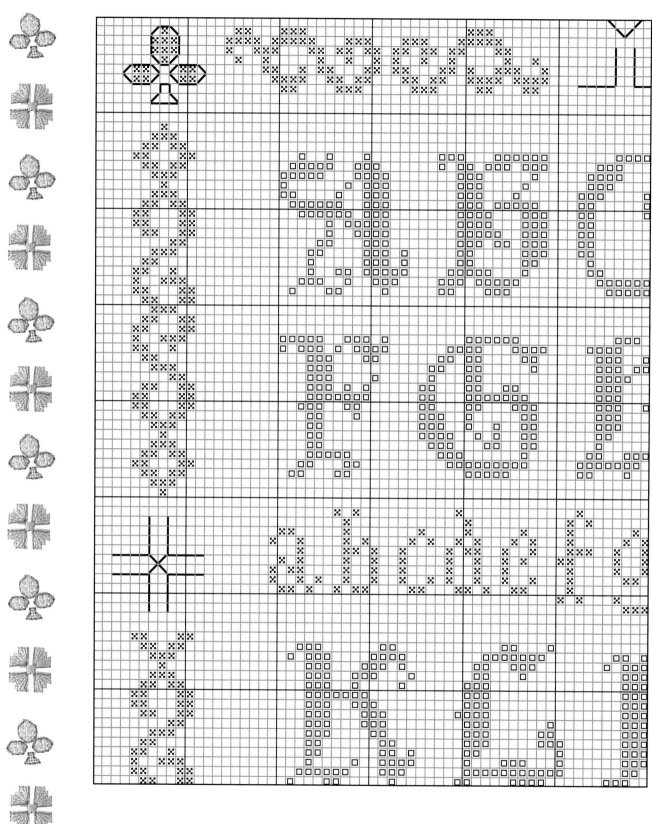

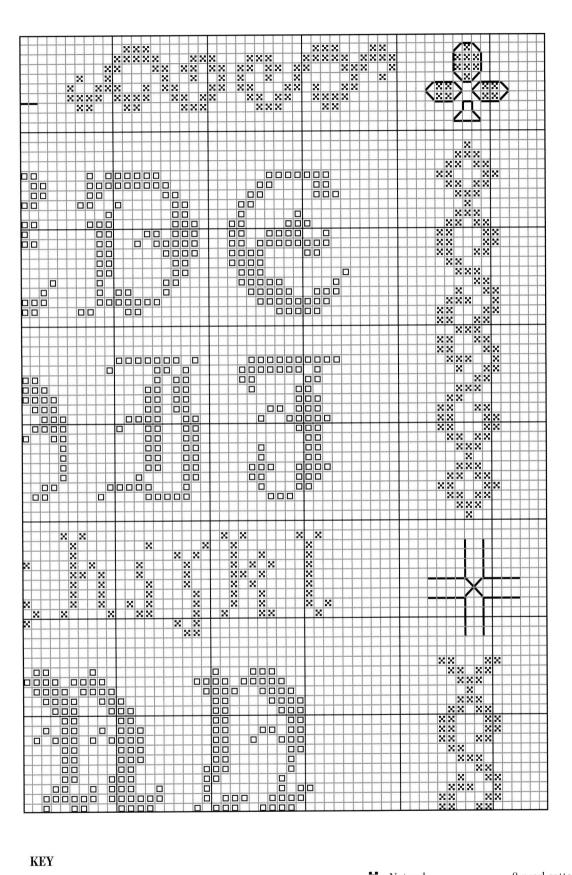

KEY TO CHART
DIVISION

page 118	page 119
page 120	page 121

KEY

□ White   8-pearl cotton

✖ Natural   8-pearl cotton DMC 739

3 Antique   stranded cotton DMC 371

Other Alphabets

The following alphabets are used in the projects to personalize your work by adding your initials and a date. However, they are also shown to provide you with alternative lettering as you develop your own designs and styles.

Alphabet 1

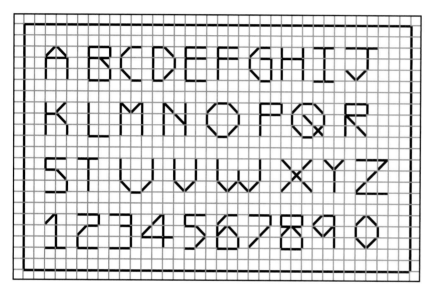

Alphabet 2

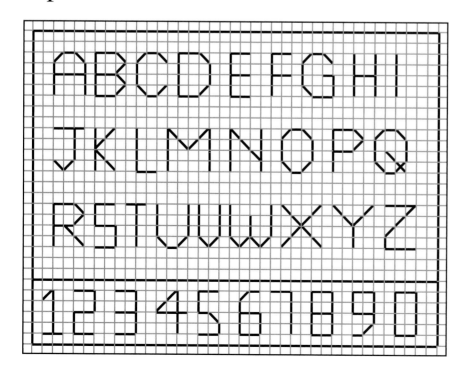

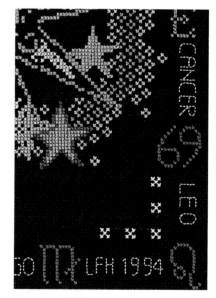

Alphabet 3

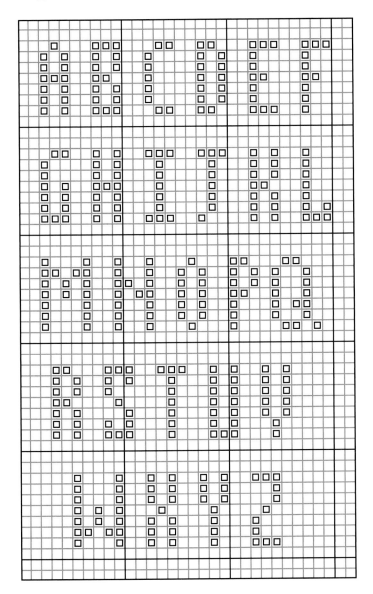

Alphabet 4

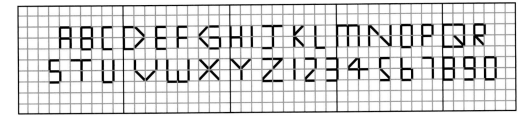

Alphabet 5

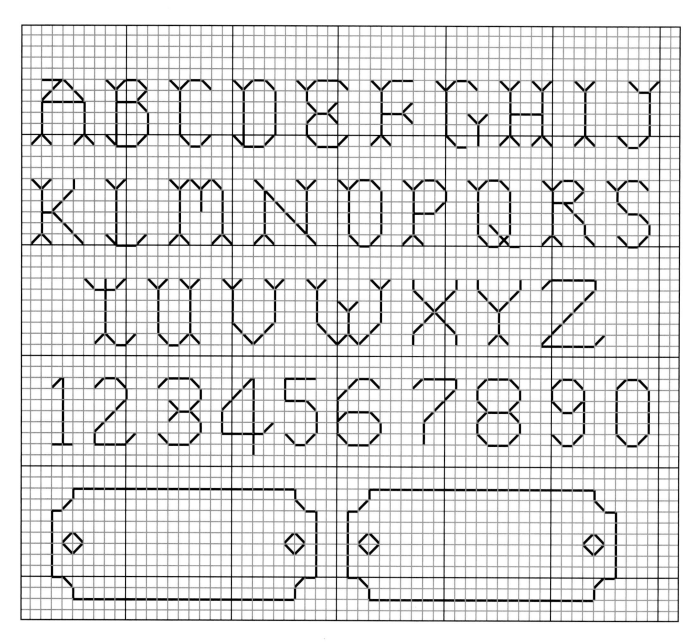

Alphabet 6

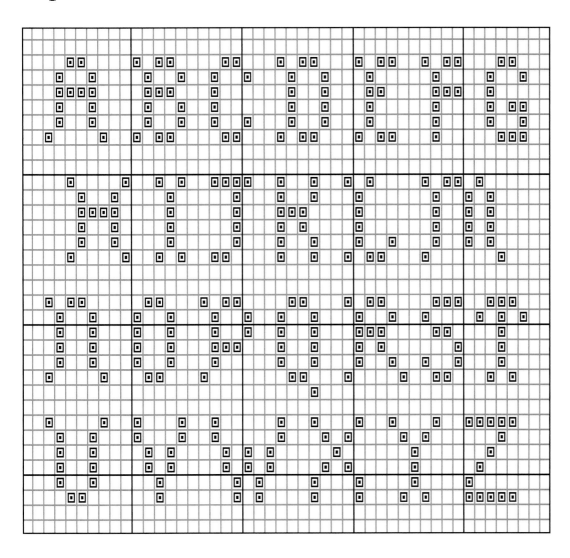

Stockists

KITS:
All the designs in this collection are available as kits from stockists or by mail order. The kits contain ready-sorted threads and all the materials necessary to complete the project. The brass charms are also available. For details write to:

Lauren Turner, Lifetime Samplers
Red Lion Cottage, 9 Vicarage Lane, Ruddington
Nottingham NG11 6HB
www.lifetimesamplers.co.uk

FABRICS:
Willow Fabrics
95 Town Lane, Mobberley, Cheshire WA16 7HH
www.willowfabrics.com

DAYLIGHT SIMULATION LAMPS:
Daylight Studios
89–91 Scrubs Lane, London NW10 6QU

THREADS:
DMC, Anchor and Madeira are widely available from needlecraft shops. The following manufacturers can advise on your nearest stockist:

DMC Creative World
62 Pullman Road, Wigston, Leics LE8 2DY

Anchor
Kilncraigs Mill, Alloa, Clackmannan FK10 1EG

Madeira Threads
Thirsk Industrial Park, York Road, Thirsk, N. Yorks YO7 3BX

GREETING CARD BLANKS:
Craft Creations Ltd
Ingersoll House, Delamare Rd, Cheshunt, Herts EN8 9ND

Index